Spiritual
GPS

NAVIGATING
IN THE
KINGDOM OF GOD

DONNA M. CASEY

ISBN 978-1-0980-5503-5 (paperback)
ISBN 978-1-0980-5504-2 (digital)

Christian Faith Publishing, Inc.
832 Park Avenue
Meadville, PA 16335
www.christianfaithpublishing.com

All scripture quotations are from the King James Version.

Printed in the United States of America

This book is dedicated to everyone whose soul cries out for a clean heart, a pure spirit, and clean hands. It is dedicated to those with an insatiable desire for truth in their inward parts. It is dedicated to those whose heart yearn to please the Lord and to truly be right before Him. It is to the people of God who understand that love must be the root of everything we do. It is to those who do not want to get in the way of the Lord being glorified to the utmost in their life. It is to those who want to walk in the true yoke-destroying, life-giving, and soul-delivering power that can only be found in Jesus. This book is dedicated to those who want directions to the secret place, which is found on the other side of the cross and in His presence. I pray this book points you to Jesus and His sovereignty and helps you to navigate victoriously through some of your toughest situations.

To the King of Kings and Lord of Lords, the only wise and sovereign God, to my Lord and Savior, Jesus Christ— thank you for loving me. May you be forever glorified.

CONTENTS

Foreword 7

Acknowledgments 9

Chapter 1: My "Why" 11

Chapter 2: Choose You This Day Who You Will Serve 25

Chapter 3: The Process: Kicking against the Pricks 36

Chapter 4: Eat the Meat and Spit out the Bones 44

Chapter 5: Pedestals 53

Chapter 6: Being Delivered from People 65

Chapter 7: Watch Your Mouth 89

Chapter 8: "Church Hurt" 99

Chapter 9: Forgiveness 114

Chapter 10: Pain into Purpose 128

Chapter 11: I'm Dying to Love You 143

Chapter 12: Die Empty 155

FOREWORD

After pastoring a local church for thirty years, I have discovered something very profound. Being a senior pastor is one of the most challenging careers, occupations, or callings a person can have. Not only do I understand this, but many others, who research careers and occupations, have come to understand the same thing. That being said, as a pastor, I use every available resource at my disposal, to assist me in fulfilling my role as a pastor. Like many pastors I read, research, and study a plethora of books that deal with a variety of subjects. One of the major subjects I endeavor to find in books I choose are those that assist me in understanding issues parishioners have. Some of these books hit the nail on the head while others don't.

That is where Donna Casey comes in. If I did not know Donna personally, after pastoring her for eleven years, I would think that she is a pastor or at least someone who researches the deep-seated issues people have. In her book, *Spiritual GPS*, Donna does an outstanding job getting to the crux of why people, as a whole, never fully become all that they are created to be. Her insight into the inner workings of the human heart, soul, and mind is nothing less than exceptional. Instead of brushing over the numerous internal problems human beings struggle with, Donna deals with them head-on in a very honest, thought-provoking, and practical way.

One of the things this book will do is cause you to look at yourself from a pragmatic and honest manner. These two important steps are vital if a person is going to get to the root of the issues that keeps them from maximizing their potential in life. I firmly believe that one of the major reasons people are mired in mediocracy is because they fail to look at themselves from an open and honest point of view. In each of the twelve chapters of her book, Donna offers hands on strategies that will assist you in reaching your life's destiny. *Spiritual GPS* is not only very practical, but it is very inspirational as well.

I encourage you to read *Spiritual GPS* and apply the principles found in it. After you do these two things, your life will change in ways you never thought possible. I highly recommend *Spiritual GPS* for anyone who is interested in taking life to "the next level." Finally, there is a resource that is designed to do just that.

—Bishop Larry J. Baylor
Senior Pastor, Faith Miracle Temple
Presiding Bishop, Higher Ground International Ministries

ACKNOWLEDGMENTS

Only God knows all the things I walked through to be able to put ink to paper and write this book, and even then, it was His strength, grace, and mercy that brought me through—all good things come from Him alone. Only the Lord has been with me in every dessert, in every valley, and in every mountaintop. So I acknowledge Jesus as my strong tower, I acknowledge Him as sovereign, and I acknowledge Him as the strength and grace that allowed me to write this book. I acknowledge that He is a promise keeper and true to His word. He is the author and finisher of my faith, the alpha and omega, and I bless Him for allowing me to fulfill purpose for His glory.

When I think of the support that fueled me to take on and complete this book, I think of my husband, Christopher. Thank you for walking through this process with me: praying, fasting, consecrating, and proofreading with me. Thank you for holding me up in prayer when I needed it most. Thank you for speaking confidence and encouragement into my spirit. This book was born just as much from your sacrifice as it was from mine. This achievement belongs to us both. I love you forever.

I wish to also thank Latricia Buckner, MA LPC. Thank you for challenging me and lighting a fire under me to not only start the book, but to finish it. Thank you for talking me through the obstacles that would have tried to hinder me from doing what the Lord was so clearly calling me to do. You were used by the Lord greatly, and you have made a significant impact on my life, more than you know. I will forever be grateful to you.

To my family and friends, thank you so much for your feedback during this process. To Trynai Braselman, Devon Haskins, Elyce Haskins, Demetrius Thomas, and Tamara Crawford-Thomas; the prayers prayed, and the encouragement given I will never forget. Thank you for sacrificing your time to support what God had given me to do.

To two of the greatest men of God that I know, Apostle Larry J. Baylor and Dr. Marlon T. Baylor, thank you for your spiritual counsel and godly leadership. Thank you for your direction during this process and willingness to help and support; it means the world to me.

To any and everyone else—who has ever given me a word, prayed for me, encouraged, supported, or simply loved me genuinely—thank you from the bottom of my heart.

CHAPTER 1

My "Why"

At the end of the day, when it is all said and done, only what we do for Christ will last. It would be tragic to live life only to discover at the end of it, the Lord says, "I never knew you: depart from me, ye that work iniquity." The Bible talks about there being a way that seems right to a man, but that at the end of that way, there is death and destruction. God is the Creator of all things. He created us for a purpose, and if we do not fulfill the purpose in which *He* intended us to fulfill; but rather, we tell the one that created us that we know better than Him, and that we had a better way, I wonder what would happen. If we really love Jesus, at some point, we must face the giant within us so that we can completely surrender to the will and way of God for our lives. The ability to do this is beyond our natural capacity. It takes a supernatural power to give us the strength and ability we need to continually be transformed into the image of Christ. We must die to our flesh and allow the spirit of God to stand up, stretch out, rule and reign in and through us.

The Holy Spirit is like the gift that keeps on giving. It has everything you need, but you must choose to receive it.

Immediately, upon reception, it gives you salvation. You dig in a little deeper, and you find peace, strength, wisdom, love, patience, joy, and so on. The more you explore and learn of the Holy Spirit (Jesus), the closer you get to Him, the more you become like Him, the more you start to think His thoughts, adapt His ways, and begin to love what He loves and hate what He hates. This is a process, and it takes time. A lot of us have died in the process. We have grown faint, got out of place, made wrong turns and, for some of us, found ourselves totally out of the will of God, all because we did not understand the process, its purpose, and because we did not know how to navigate in the kingdom of God. Thanks be to Jesus that we serve a God that can resurrect what was once dead.

The most comprehensive and exhaustive book on "the process" is the *Bible*, which is the Word of God, the Basic Instructions Before Leaving Earth. It is essential that we read God's Word and not only read it but meditate on it, and not only meditate on it and rehearse it in our mind so that it can seep into our spirit, but we must apply His Word. We must live His Word.

Sometimes the practical application or understanding of what this looks like escapes us for one reason or another. Sometimes life and situations can hit us hard, and it is not that we don't know the Word of God, but trials and tribulations can drown out the Word that we know, and we may need to be reminded—reminded of God's Word, what it says about our situation, and not only our situation, but what it says about who He is in us and who we are to be in Him.

Sometimes, our thinking just needs a slight adjustment. We need a course correction to help us come back into proper alignment with God, His Word, and His will for our life. Prayerfully, this book can serve as a reference manual and a possible companion to the Word regarding everyday situations.

This book was born out of hardship, trials, suffering, and unrelenting love for Jesus. It was born out of a desire to help people get close to God no matter what is going on and a desire to help people endure so they can get through to the other side of the test, experience sweet victory and intimacy with God which brings about a freedom that is unmatched. I wanted to help us not turn away from God when times get hard and our emotions are raging, but rather, lean into God to find that hiding place in Him where safety and shelter reside.

God says in Romans 8:28 that all things work together for the good to them that love God, to them that are called according to His purpose. God is so gracious that He uses our experiences (good and bad) and works them for our good (that is to all who love Him, and to them that are called according to His purpose).

I believe, that if you are reading this book, this applies to you. Ultimately, in everything that has ever happened to me, or because of me… I either learned what to do or what not to do. Sometimes, you don't understand why you are going through something until God shows you that what you went through was to help someone else.

God impregnated me with this book years ago, and I am just now ready to put my fingers to the keyboard. I have prayed, fasted, consecrated, and listened. The nudge in my spirit was so unbearable that I knew it was time to write. Every time I turned around, the Lord would send someone to ask me if I had written the book yet. This book is the fulfillment of the Word of the Lord that He gave to me in prayer and that had been prophesied to me on multiple occasions. So here it is.

I asked God to write through me and to speak to His people as only He can. It is only His anointing that destroys the yoke. So I pray that God does what He does best: heal, deliver, and set free. I pray that He reveal, give insight, empower, encourage, catapult, revive, restore, and strengthen. I hope this book can offer a different perspective on situations that will give us the strength to endure and go through so that God can be glorified. My hope is that the sovereignty of God seeps through in every chapter. My heart is that we would fall even more in love with God, that we would become even more intimately acquainted with Him.

I now understand why I had to take the road that I did. Now granted, some things I experienced were because of bad decisions that I made, wrong mindsets, and skewed vision. And God had to heal, destroy yokes, loose chains, and cast down strongholds. Other times, the suffering had nothing to do with my decisions at all. It was in those times I felt what I was going through was unfair. I literally thought I must have been one of God's least favorite. To be honest, at times, I struggled with if God could ever love me at all, much less try to believe that I was the apple of His eye. I thought He tolerated me, I thought I was a mishap…but that is because that is what I grew up feeling.

However, God is not like man. He is a good, good Father. What I came to understand is that God was going to use me for His glory. And the suffering was the shedding process. It was the process in which He was making me more like Him, and in turn, the process would bless many others.

I came to understand that just because something hurts, it does not necessarily mean that it is a bad thing. If someone is sick and they need an operation, the doctor may need to cut on them to remove whatever is causing the illness, or he may need to cut them to go in and fix whatever the source of the issue is. After the surgery, the patient may be in a lot of pain, but the operation was to heal whatever was going on with the person. The expectation is that after the patient has had time to recover, they would feel better and be healed completely. Now, that is if they healed properly. Normally, after surgery, the doctor would give care instructions to the patient on what they need to do in order to help the healing process along so they can heal appropriately. If all goes well, and the doctor made no mistakes, the operation would be deemed a success. Even though pain was experienced, the expected outcome outweighed the need to avoid the pain. **The pain was necessary.**

How great is it to know that the doctor who operates on us is the master physician, who makes no mistakes. He doesn't cause any frivolous pain, and every operation He ever performed was a hundred percent successful. He is the only doctor that cannot fail.

God is sovereign. He's all knowing. He knows how much we can take. If we are in Him and He is in us, no amount of pressure—pain—or persecution is unbearable. It's not unbearable because we have a strength within us that is made perfect in our weakness. When our strength is depleted, the strength of Jesus stands up. Even when we feel as if we cannot take any more, *if* we are going about this journey the way His Word instructs, we will *always* be okay. **Every time!** No matter what. We will always get through it. We will always come out on the other side. **Every time!** That is, if we are leaning into Him.

The problem exists when we back off instead of pressing into Jesus. We can't allow our struggles to estrange us from the one that has power over what we are facing. One of the reasons I believe we don't press into God like we should when we are going through is because of a lack of understanding. **Sometimes we just don't understand the "why."** However, in this walk…even when we don't understand why we are going through it, we are to trust. But this can be hard. In certain situations, we seem to trust God wholeheartedly, and in other areas, we don't. But our trust in God must become consistent and unshakable—in every area.

For some of us, developing that type of trust was, and sometimes still is a process.

For me, the interesting part is while walking through certain situations, God often allowed me to be very aware of what was going on. I didn't get to be oblivious. No, He allowed me to feel every bit of it as it was crushing me. When He was killing pride in me so that humility could manifest, He allowed me to have insight into what was going on and why. He allowed situations to come that would test and kill what He was trying to remove. When He was chipping away at the hardness of my heart so that compassion could come forth, He let me understand exactly what was going on. The process of removing a stony heart and the Lord giving you a heart of flesh, one that is softened to what He wills, is an anguishing and excruciating process when there is no anesthesia to numb the pain. He allowed me to be privy to the inner workings of this deliverance process.

It brought me to my knees, but it was the catalyst to cultivating and nurturing the most intimate relationship I have ever had and will ever have—and that is my relationship with Jesus. Suffering has a way of bringing you closer to God if you let it serve its purpose. He needed me to grow and mature. I was being molded into what He called me to be. It hurt, but it was for my good. We must be malleable to God's will without anything restricting or blocking Him from moving through us. **And "IF" you ever told God "YES," if you told Him that He could use you for His glory, He is coming after everything that would hinder that from happening.** It is up to you to submit it to Him, but He will definitely require it of you.

For instance, there was a season when I was favored and was sought out because of the gifts God put in me. Then the very next season, I was rejected. I felt tossed to the side and unwanted. I was in a place where I felt like no one liked me, no one understood me, people looked down on me, and God allowed me to feel every bit of that. I went from being over-confident to losing confidence. God allowed this because my compassion had waxed cold, pride needed to die, and humility needed to reign if I was ever going to truly be used by Him and be a vessel of honor. So, I had to decide whether I would go on the potter's wheel surrendering or if I would go kicking and screaming. During this process, I did struggle…a lot. The devil was trying to kill my will to go on; he was trying to steal my strength and destroy my purpose. Meanwhile, at the same time, God was trying to get me to submit to His process which was to kill my flesh so that He could use me for His glory. God WON! In all our lives, the devil is trying to accomplish something, and God is trying to accomplish something. Who will you let win? God never loses; the victory is always guaranteed when you abide in Jesus. The only time you will ever lose is if you come from up under His protection…and that is where the enemy is waiting for you.

See, in the times that I was in the valley, the devil wanted to end my life and get me to give up while I was down because he knows that **if we come to ourselves and allow Jesus to stand up in us, it is over!** His whole plan is to get us out of the will of God so that we can forfeit the blessing God has for us. Even though it hurt, I now understand why I had to go through what I went through. **But what if I had died in the process? Or given up in the process? I wouldn't have been here to write this book.**

See, I was at a pivotal moment in my life. I was at a cross-roads. In my spirit destiny and purpose was calling, but in my flesh, discouragement, tiredness, and fear were trying to overtake me. I had to decide, once and for all, was I going to let the cares of this life swallow me up whole and spit me out to die with my purpose being unfulfilled and being buried in the grave with me? Or was I going to declare that I shall live and not die to declare the work of the Lord? I had to decide to press through, believe God and what I knew He called me to do even if what I felt was totally contrary. Was I going to cower and give in to the insurmountable and overwhelming weight of doubt and fear, or was I going to finally submit my way to God's way completely and totally surrender to the one whose perfect love cast out all fear?

The enemy tried to tell me because of having experienced countless battles—that I did not have enough fortitude, spiritual tenacity, bounce back, emotional or spiritual energy, or strength left to push through…BUT THE DEVIL IS A LIE! Obviously, he did not win that battle because here we are, you are reading the book God gave me…and the same goes for you. You will go forth and conquer!

Yes, I was depleted and weak, but the enemy must have forgot, or at least he hoped, that I forgot that God's strength is made perfect in my weakness. So even when I am weak, because of JESUS, I am yet strong. And this is what we must fight to always remember. Greater is He that is in us than he that is in the world.

The devil wants to mess us up before purpose can be fulfilled. God was gutting out everything in me that would even think about mishandling the anointing and gift on my life. God would help me to see myself, my heart, the erroneous perceptions in my mind. He would show me how I was operating out of faulty thinking rather than His love or His truth of who He was in me and who I was in Him.

What it all boiled down to was: I WAS STILL BROKEN. I still had unforgiveness buried in my soul; I still had the negativity spoken over my life running on repeat in my thoughts; I had yet to remove all the knives in my back, not to mention the regrets lingering in my heart. See, I had pushed it so far down; I thought because it was unseen, it was gone. But nothing was further from the truth. And on top of all that mess and brokenness that was never healed, I piled on the knowledge of God and my experiences in church that I thought meant maturity in God. But I was building on a broken foundation.

See, because hurt, rejection, distrust, unforgiveness, and disappointment were mixed in with the building materials of this structure that "I had built," the devil had the ability to destroy it at any given time. **So the bricks that were laid on shaky ground had to be torn down so that God could build it back upon a firm foundation**. Jesus wanted the building gutted and the foundation relaid. The only indestructible building is one built on the Word of God, on faith, on hope, on love, on humility, on forgiveness, on Jesus! It does not matter how many theology degrees we have; if our house is built on an unstable foundation, it will come down.

I knew that God had anointed me, but the restraint, the love, the discipline, the integrity to act according to the will of God and not the will of Donna when things got tough had not caught up to the anointing on my life. So God had to tear me down to build me back up again…in Him. It was important for me to include this because this is where the passion for this book comes from. **And it is in this part of the process where many of us get lost, confused, or become hopeless and we start to make mistakes.** It is because we cannot discern what is really going on. And we don't know how to navigate through rough terrain. We self-diagnose what is occurring in our life. **God is breaking us to make us, but we believe that God is punishing us.** Even His correction is out of love.

The Bible says He chastises those whom He loves. God loves us so much that if we let Him… He will refuse to allow us to stay broken. And He loves us so much that He will refuse to allow you to continue bleeding on people because you are broken or because your character hasn't matured to the level of the anointing on your life. Broken doesn't just mean you have been hurt or are in despair. If you are prideful, you are broken. If you lack confidence in the God that lives in you, then something, somewhere is broken. If you misuse and abuse the gifts and call on your life, something in you is broken. If you are arrogant, you are broken. God wants to make us whole in Him in every area, and sometimes within that process…we get off track.

I have personally gone through and witnessed many different situations where deliverance, course correction, or just proper insight were needed. It is the wisdom gained in those experiences that I pray unveils itself in this book. The lessons, revelations, and knowledge acquired in those situations will prayerfully help deliver us from some faulty thinking. I kicked against the pricks many times in this walk. I have seen others make catastrophic mistakes, and I would think... if only they realized what was going on. If only they could see what was happening in the spirit. If only they could see how the enemy was manipulating the situation, playing them like a puppet and using their own emotions and lack of understanding to do it. I would think, "If only they understood." I could see it so clearly, not only because of the insight that God has given me, but because I, too, had allowed the same thing to happen to me at one time or another.

For many years, the enemy tried to silence me, but he has failed. This book is a reclamation of the voice that God gave me. He called me to speak for Him; He anointed me to see. Just like the enemy has attempted with you...he tried all he could to get you out of place, distract you, cause you to forfeit the blessing and call that is on your life. But God! Jesus said NOT SO, and what the devil thought he was doing to kill you... God was allowing to make you. YES, it was killing your flesh so that the spirit of God could rule and reign in you and through you, but it was strengthening and fortifying your spirit.

I know what it feels like to make mistakes; I know what it felt like to be lost, to be hurt, to be broken, to be depressed, to be misunderstood, to be targeted, to be disappointed and let down, to be weary in well-doing, to be burned-out in church, to be offended, to be the offender, and to be ostracized and rejected. I know what it felt like to have people look down on you. I also am very aware of the wisdom, the growth, the strength that can be gained if we would just go through without trying to forgo the process. If we would just walk it out with God and learn what we need to learn, we can turn what we think are losses into wins. However, I am equally aware of what the enemy tries to do when you are in those vulnerable situations and how he tries to capitalize on a moment of weakness, hurt, disappointment, and confusion. The enemy uses distraction, ignorance, emotion, and our fleshly desires against us. It is my heart to help us recognize the enemy's devices and to **also identify the enemy within** so that we don't end up helping our adversary destroy us.

Even though you and I know what pain feels like, JESUS KNOWS more than us all. We want to know the enemy's tactics, but more importantly, we need to be looking for the will of God, the opportunities to grow and become more like Him, and love like Him. Not love as we suppose in our natural mind, but love as outlined in the Scriptures. We will get to that later in the book. But within these pages, my prayer is that the sovereignty of God will shine through, and while reading, you will begin to recognize it in your life. Ultimately, that is what matters.

I walked through a lot of things alone, just me and Jesus. There were many times where I had no one in my corner, no one that would pour into me, and no one that would fight for me. While I was hurt by it at the time, it worked out for my good, and in hindsight, I wouldn't have it any other way unless I would have learned the same lessons and acquired and tapped into the same anointing on my life that I have now. So as I write, it is not out of regret—but joy, and that's because I now see why it was necessary. While I was in it and going through…it broke me…but that is where I needed to be. "The sacrifices of God are **a broken** spirit: **a broken** and a

contrite heart, O God, thou wilt not despise" (Psalm 51:17; emphasis mine).

I had to go to God for everything because I didn't have many people to talk to that could help me navigate through church culture, people, trials, this walk, and all that comes with it, but God would use all of that to help me write this book. I pray it helps you. I realized, after being saved for twenty years now, that seasoned saints and leaders could benefit from a book like this as well as those still trying to find their way. I know because I have talked to many leaders: pastors, prophets, evangelist, and teachers who needed someone to talk to about various situations—someone to bounce their thinking off on and talk things out with, someone they could trust, and someone who could understand.

Ultimately it is the understanding and insight that comes from God that can help us. I prayed that God would breathe on this book and anoint its pages. I pray that God would infuse each chapter with revelation, insight, and yoke-destroying power—the kind of power that illuminates the mind and increases the ability to hold a greater capacity of understanding that can only come from Jesus.

This is not meant to be a "one size fits all" kind of deal. In every situation, the best advice anyone could ever give is to listen to God and obey what He says. You can have two people going through the same situation and God gives different directives to them both. Even in that, you will find that He may have given different solutions but they both will line up with His Word. The problem enters when there is a discrepancy between what people are saying God said and what He actually said…either through His written Word or through a rhema word.

Many people say that God told them this and He told them that, but some of this stuff people are saying God said is against His Word and is contrary to common sense. So this book is meant to course-correct if we have veered a little too far to the left or right in our thinking as it relates to how God would have us handle certain situations. Even though I am relating this to the church, a lot of these principles can be used in our workplace and in our own relationships.

So get ready to go on a journey. Each chapter delves deeper and deeper. We deal with the basics, and then we dig a little further. With each chapter, with the help of the Lord, we are chipping away at erroneous thinking, strongholds in our mind and in our spirit, and prayerfully aligning our thoughts and mind with the thoughts of God. This book is meant to offer a different perspective and insight that may give you the strength to either endure, change, embrace, empower, receive healing, or all the above. Only the anointing destroys yokes, and I am fully aware that deliverance is not obtained through power or might, but only by the Spirit of the Lord. With this on my heart, **I pray God speaks to you through the words on these pages and does what only He can do!**

CHAPTER 2

Choose You This Day
Who You Will Serve

Before we go any further and embark on this journey, I feel compelled to put a chapter in the book for those who had not completely surrendered themselves to Jesus, or to those who are struggling with the decision to do so. Prayerfully, you will make your choice today. I am very aware that we can attend church but not be "in" the church, or rather, the church not be in us. Jesus is looking for those who will worship Him in spirit AND in truth.

So this part of the book is dedicated to those who are still searching, to those who are afraid of the unknown, to those who feel as if you cannot live holy, to those who feel like you must get it together before you come into the church, to those who think you won't have as much fun if you come into the kingdom. It is to those who feel like you will have to change the way you do things; it is to those who feel that you will have too many restraints and rules. The truth is, there is a void in everyone that can only be filled by God. For the rest of your life, you will seek things out to fill this void, whether it be love from people, relationships, validation, career, money, drugs, alcohol, and so on. But none of those things will ever satiate your soul like JESUS, and if you would be honest with yourself, you must admit that there is something aching inside of you for greater. No matter how you try to silence it, the void inside of you will cry out in unexpected ways.

I tried to fill my void with men. See, I did not grow up in a religious household. I never really knew what home felt like, and I didn't have much direction. Whatever values I learned, I picked up from observation along the way. I didn't know my worth, and I was looking for love in all the wrong places and from all the wrong people. I did not know who I was, and I certainly didn't know anything about living holy. I was searching for something deeper; I wanted to be better. I knew it had to be something more to life than what I knew. I didn't know then, but that was God dealing with me. So I started reading self-help books. I'd decided I would become a better person. So I attempted to stop smoking, cursing, and drinking, among other things. It is important to note here that even though I stopped on my own…most likely if I had run into a difficult situation or hard times, I would have reverted…because only the power of God truly delivers. So while I was able to stop those things for a time, there were other things that weren't so easy to part with.

I was eighteen years old when I started going to church with my aunt. She had gotten saved a few years earlier, and I was a witness to how it totally changed her life. I knew nothing at all about God, but if He could do for me what He did for my aunt, I wanted in. I had always talked about Jesus, but I did not know Him. The more I went to church, the more I wanted to go. Now you wouldn't have been able to tell if you were observing me with natural eyes because I would come in the church, and people would hug me and show me so much love, but it was uncomfortable and awkward to me. I didn't know how to receive it. I would be thinking, "Get off of me," yet deep down inside, I craved it. I had a hard exterior. Worship would be going on, and I would just sit there. I would not sing a word, I would not clap, and I would not stand up. COLD as ice on the outside, but on the inside, something was breaking. There was something intriguing about seeing people cry before the Lord, dance without a care of who was looking, speaking a language I did not understand, and jumping around as free as a bird. I tried to act like it was all too much, but really, I wished I had the courage to be as free as they seemed to be, but I was in bondage, **screaming so loudly in the silence,** wanting to be free, but not knowing how to go about it. Back then I thought I was too cute to jump around. I didn't want to mess up my hair...but really, I thought I would look silly doing it. I didn't understand... but I kept coming back. I was yearning for something deeper on the inside. I was battling, **trying to hold on to the world while reaching out for Jesus**.

The Bible says that a double-minded man is unstable in all his ways (James 1:8). When we first decide to start seeking after God, the world is going to fight hard to not let you go. Your flesh is going to fight even harder not to lose its control over you. The fleshly desires will try to intensify. What is happening is the enemy and your flesh are trying to diminish the effect that this newfound influence is having on you. The enemy and your flesh will try and work together to make you feel as if the changes that you will make to follow God are unattainable...but fight through it. He is a liar and your flesh is too. The enemy fears when you are anchored in God, so He tries to get you before you really learn of God and His power, and before you learn who you are in Him.

See, I wanted God, but I didn't know how to come out from among the world. Before receiving the Holy Spirit, I would go to church and come out feeling all inspired and determined to make a change. I would be ready to give it all up for Jesus, then "he" would call and ask me to go out to the movies. "He" would tell me that he missed me, and he realized he needed me in his life and can't see a future without me.

"He" is someone I thought was the love of my life. We had been broken up for years, but right when I started going to church, here "he" came.

Do not fall for the enemies' tactics. Ask yourself, "Why now?" Why is that man or that woman ready to finally make it right with you now? Why are these people coming out of the woodwork now? Why is this job that is going to pay you more than you ever made but will keep you from going to church regularly coming at this specific time in your life? Why is it coming at a time where you are at a crossroads, at a time where you are deciding to give your life to God? If the enemy, who HATES YOU, is trying to reward you and buy your soul to prevent you from giving your life and heart to Jesus wholeheartedly, have you asked yourself what would happen if you didn't fall victim to his plot to stop you from making the best decision you could ever make in your life?

What if you were determined to get to God no matter what you had to give up? What if none of the enemy's strategies worked against you? What if you decided to pursue God until you were filled with His spirit? That is what the enemy does not want, and he will do whatever he can, give whatever he can, to prevent you from following through with your decision. But think about this: he will not give you too much; he is only going to give you just enough for you to make the wrong decision. Whatever he thinks, it will cost for you to stay under his influence. If your price is a man or a woman, he will send them to you. If your price is just getting out of poverty and giving you businesses and money so that you serve "it" instead of God…then you may just get what you want…but the enemy is counting on HELL to be your portion. DO NOT LET HIM DO THIS TO YOU. He does not want to lose control over you, your mind, or soul. In actuality, it really is not about you; he is just using you to try and hurt God; you are just a pawn in the grand scheme of things. So what will you do?

There is a big misconception that people have as it relates to when to come to God. I have heard many people say that they wanted to stop sinning, they wanted to stop sleeping around, they wanted to stop cursing, drinking, smoking, lying, or what have you before they came to church. This is a big mistake. See, even though you may still be doing those things, the only thing that can help you stop is the power of God, His Spirit. And every time you find yourself in His house, the word is chipping away at the bondage that you are in.

When I first started going to church at eighteen years old, I was still sleeping with men that were not my husband. I had stopped other things, but the power to stop getting myself into relationships that were not good for me escaped me. However, I was going to church. I had not yet been filled with His spirit, but I wanted it. I even started to pray and asked God to fill me. I would go to church and decide I would not talk to another guy. The more and more I got into God and His Word, the more and more strength I gained.

I was still struggling, but I was determined to pursue God until I got Him. I came to Him how I was: I was in sin. He was the only one that could help me. Every time I came into His house, He was dealing with me. God was chipping away; the Word was getting in me and doing things in my heart and mind that I could not see. I had stopped doing a lot of things, but there was something still holding me back from fully receiving God. No matter how many things I had stopped doing on my own, utter and total deliverance can only come from Jesus. I did not have the power to deliver myself completely. So I continued to struggle because I was still trying to hold on to this one thing while pursuing God.

That one thing…

I remember the straw that broke the camel's back. It was New Year's Eve, and "he," the ex-boyfriend who I thought I was so in love with, wanted to spend the night with me. (That always happens when you set your mind to do right; the enemy devises tactics to stop and distract you, and it will work if you let it). The enemy knew I had a soul tie to this individual. Years earlier, I was pregnant with our baby, and if I hadn't lost it, he would have been the father of our child, so that hold over me was strong. All I could ever get out of him when we were in a relationship and when I was pregnant were donuts and orange juice. Now years later, he finally gets some sort of revelation that he wants to be with me and now is trying to woo me with drinks, dinner, and a hotel room. Was that all my soul was worth? The hotel wasn't even three stars. Matter of fact, it was a motel.

The devil doesn't value us. He finds pleasure in degrading us and humiliating us. He tries to make you worse off than what you already are when you play in his backyard.

By this time, I had been going to church for about a year and a half now. Something kept drawing me back to that church even though I did not understand everything that was going on. I had been up to the altar about twenty times by this point and could never completely let go and give my life to God all the way so that He could fill me with His spirit. Something was holding me back. AND THIS IS WHAT IT WAS. As I laid in the bed, in a motel with this boy who I realized didn't know me, and who I had no real connection with, I felt extremely empty, void, hollowed out, and lonely. This was God at work! This was the effect of all those times I had gone to church. The Word got into my heart, and it was working. See, as he attempted to carry out what we both knew we were there to do, his touch repulsed me, and nothing felt right. That night was terrible, and an incredible regret and sorrow came over me. This had never happened before.

After that incident, I found myself in church on a Sunday. The first lady of the church was preaching, and suddenly, I started crying. That was not like me; I didn't cry or show emotion in church, but on that day, the tears poured out uncontrollably. I could not stop them. About thirty minutes later, I am getting up off the floor, and everybody around me was celebrating. I had spoken in a language that I did not know; I felt a joy that I had never felt before, and I felt as light as a feather. I had finally been filled with the Holy Spirit. The enemy tried to distract and cause me to detour, but God had other plans for me. There was no other man that the devil could have used at that time that I would have wanted to be with more than the one he had used to set a snare for me on New Year's Eve.

For years after I lost my child, I still thought I was in love with the father. But when presented with what I thought

I wanted most, it did not satisfy me; as a matter of fact, it made me sick. **I realized in that motel room that I wanted God more than anything else.** Before coming to this understanding, I wasn't ready to fully give my life to God because I thought I wanted something else more than Jesus. And that was what was holding me back all that time. God wants all of you, and in return… He will love you and bless you in ways that you cannot imagine.

He means it when He says put no other gods before Him. That means, no lovers, no hurt, no disappointment, no regret, no unforgiveness, no money, no job, no drugs, no alcohol, no gang, no social group, no person, no place, and no thing can be LORD in your life.

When God knows that you will submit everything to Him and let go of WHATEVER He instructs you to, then you are ready…then all hindrances are removed. Then the house can be swept clean. Nothing is hiding or hanging on and God can come in and occupy and fill every space with Himself.

Truth is, it can be a little scary when embracing a new way of living, but I tell you what: if you find the courage to push through and pursue, you will spend the rest of your life thanking God that you did. Truth is, no one can live holy in their own power alone. It takes the power of God's Spirit to help you. Our righteousness is as of filthy rags, but if we put on the righteousness of Christ, HIS BLOOD can wash away our sins and make us white as snow, by faith and grace through and in Christ Jesus. So trying to stop smoking, lying, and fornicating before you come to church because you don't want to be a hypocrite is like trying to heal yourself at home from a gunshot wound before you go to the hospital. Do you get what I am saying?

You go to the hospital so that the doctors can operate on you. You don't have the knowledge nor skill to know how to treat that gunshot wound. Same thing, when you say you must get right before you can go to church. **No**, you go to church so that you can get right. The truth is, I have had way more fun since I have been in the kingdom than when I was not. Plus I have fun that I don't have to pay for or repent for later. Truth is, if you want God, you will have to change the way you do things, and if you are not willing to, then you are not ready to discover the best version of yourself; you are not ready to be blessed beyond measure; you are not ready to discover what your God-given purpose is because if you want all of this, you have to get it God's way by following and submitting to Him. Truth is that the rules and restraints are because He loves you. The rules are to protect us from the enemy, the world, and ourselves…and if you don't want a God that loves you like that…keep searching for the counterfeit. Keep chasing after void fillers, but it will only leave you empty and wanting.

When you get sick and tired of being sick tired, then you are ready. Hopefully, it will not be too late by the time you decide to try God. We can't be LORD over our own life because we are not sovereign, all-knowing, nor all-powerful. Our knowledge is limited. We don't know our beginning from our end; we can't give ourselves joy, peace, or salvation. All good things come from God. We don't control anything, and if God wants His breath back, then we cease to live. If He decides to take the body back that your spirit is housed in, then certainly a burial is in your near future. The thing is, we have a God that died for our sins so that He could redeem us, restore us, save us, love us, use us for His glory, and we reject Him. Yet we are sometimes quicker to embrace a man or woman that means us no good and will fight to keep them in our lives, when the one who created you both is waiting for you to just let Him in.

He is waiting to open your eyes and show you His love for you and how it was Him that has been keeping you. It was His grace and mercy that He extended to you that spared your life or kept you from a nervous breakdown or helped you recover from one. It was Him…it has always been Him.

The way this world is, and with all that is going on… wouldn't it be nice to know that you had a hiding place? A safe place you could go to lay all your burdens down? A place you could go where you would never be misunderstood, and as a matter of fact, a place where you could go where you would even find out things about yourself that you didn't know or understand? Wouldn't it be nice to have a relationship with the one who loves you like no other ever could, the one that knows you inside and out? Wouldn't it be nice to talk to the God that created you and find out what He hid inside of you? Don't you want to know what He smuggled in the earth through you? No spouse, no boyfriend or girlfriend, no baby momma or baby daddy, no son or daughter, no mother or father, no job, no money, no food, no drugs, or alcohol can console, comfort, and love you like God. None of those things can reach as deep as Jesus can. He can touch depths of your soul, mind, and spirit that have never been revealed, places in you that you don't even know is there. He is the wisest man you will ever know. He is the solution to every problem and the answer to this dark world. Won't you try Him?

You don't have to know anything about church. You don't have to know the Bible; you don't have to know a single scripture. You don't have to own a single dress or suit. All you must do is be ready to accept Jesus in your life. All you must be is tired of doing things your way; all you have to be is willing to give Jesus a chance. All you must have is a heart that wants to be right even if you can't find the strength to do what is right. If you genuinely want Jesus, for real, eventually, you will find that He will give you the strength to let go of whatever would hinder you from letting Him in. You don't have to be perfect; you just need to be willing and sincere. It won't all change overnight, and that is okay. Step by step, day by day, start with a decision—a decision to say yes to God and mean it. And if your YES was true, God will lead you on what to do next. Ask Him to order your steps, and He will. Ultimately, if your heart is sincere, God will direct you exactly where you are supposed to be. It doesn't matter what you've done. Just repent and ask God to forgive you and to guide you. He loves you, and He is waiting on you. Call upon Him while there is still time. Surrender to Jesus completely and watch Him bless you beyond measure. "Seek ye the Lord while he may be found, call ye upon him while he is near" (Isaiah 55:6).

CHAPTER 3

The Process:
Kicking against the Pricks

The spiritual parallel of an eagle's shedding or molting process compared to the transformation process that you and I go through in life are quite similar.

When reading about eagles, I learned that their survival is linked to its plumage (feathers). They help to protect and transport them among other things. Their feathers sometimes become worn out and weakened by a buildup of oil and dirt. With a wingspan of up to eight feet, their feathers need to be light so that they can soar (fly), and they need to be strong and tight to insulate the eagles from the cold and wet. This explains their need to molt (shed the oily, dirty, and heavy feathers to make way for new ones to grow).

During this molting process, an eagle can become extremely weak. Oftentimes they cannot fly or hunt because they lose a lot of their primary and secondary feathers, and it takes a lot of energy for them to grow back. Eagles are in great danger during this period and are less able to fight disease or stress. In their weakened state, they are also in danger from predators, elements, and they can no longer tear which impairs their vision.

At some point in the molting process, the older, more mature eagles (who have experienced molting before) drop meat to the weakened eagle so that their energy can be replenished. However, not every eagle makes it through the molting or regrowth process. Those that can endure the process eventually gain enough strength to fly to a mountain. With their new feathers and renewed strength, the eagles are stronger than ever before; they rise with the ability to soar into higher realms than before the molting process. They fly against the wind which helps them to tear, and their vision is restored even clearer.

Just like the eagle, sometimes we become weakened and need to shed feathers so we can grow new ones. Our life experiences and its effect on our mind, heart, and spirit take a toll and weigh us down, resulting in our progress and growth being impeded. Through situations that have happened to us in our past, we develop defense mechanisms, set up unhealthy strongholds, and form faulty perspectives in which we filter everything through. We, like the eagle, need a molt season to remove everything that hinders us from soaring in God. Hence the PROCESS.

It has always amazed me how multifaceted God is. I would often ponder on how He could take a single situation and accomplish so many different things out of it. See, the process is not only to remove and shed things but also to prepare you for what is to come. The process equips you with what you need for the assignment and/or blessing that is waiting on the other side of the process.

Process is defined as a series of actions or steps taken in order to achieve an end. In other words, as this relates to us…we are born with a purpose, and there are situations and experiences that will come about in our life that are used to equip and move us toward fulfilling that purpose.

However, there normally is a battle that ensues when we try to get to where we need to be (destination) from where we are (starting point). It's the distance between those two locations that we have a hard time with. We don't know for certain how we are going to get from point A to point B. This results in us taking left and right turns when God is trying to get us to go straight. We all know that the shortest distance between two points is a straight line, but because we fight the process or try to forgo it altogether, we veer off course. It would behoove us to realize that we will keep going in circles and repeat the same test over and over until we finally decide to give in and embrace the process. Then and only then will TRUE progress be made.

There is so much to say about this, but I can't go into it all in this book. But I will say this: the Bible talks about a way that seems right to us, but the end of that way is death or destruction. There is only one way to successfully live and accomplish God's purpose for our lives, and that is God's way. A lot of what the process is designed to do is teach you how to submit your way (all your ways) and your will to God's will.

Oftentimes, because we don't understand what is going on in our lives, we hold God responsible for some of the poor choices we made, poor choices other people made that affected us, or we blame God for things that the enemy orchestrated. A lot of times, God is not behind the painful situations that happen to us, but He does allow it. We don't realize though that if God allowed it (and we love Him and are called according to His purpose), then it is a part of the process, and it is working for our good.

We kick against the pricks because of a lack of understanding or just outright refusal to submit to the will of God. We struggle with His sovereignty, when all He is trying to do is remove the things that don't belong, impart the things that do and teach and equip us in the process to help others and bless us for doing so, all the while developing **depth of integrity** which **determines capacity.**

What we fail to understand in the process is this: sometimes working for our good means that God leaves us right in the middle of a trying situation while holding us up so we can feel the pain and take it without buckling. **Pain can be a great tool for growth**. We are just being molded. When you were a child, and if you ever touched the stove while it was hot, then you understand this concept. The pain from touching that stove was an indicator that something was wrong, and most likely…it was the pain that kept you from ever doing it again. Thus, lesson learned. Even though the oven light or fire on the stove intrigued you, you learned just because you want to touch or experience something doesn't mean you should, or that it is good for you. So you learned caution and restraint.

God is the Potter, and we are the clay.

We are on the wheel, and quite frankly, the process can hurt. It can be uncomfortable, and sometimes it can leave you lost in translation (or so you think). However, God knows right where you are. The process is not just about learning from things that we have done wrong or removing things that are not right in us.

The other part of this process is God preparing you and fitting you for the blessings you will receive and the anointing that you will operate in. He is trying to increase your faith; otherwise, you'll never step out. He is trying to increase your capacity to hold a greater weight of glory and, at the same time, teach you how to responsibly handle and sustain what He has for you. He is trying to purify your heart so that you can see yourself as He sees you (as a GIANT in Him). He is trying to move us from a place of infancy to maturity so that we can quit fighting against Him and start cooperating with Him even when it doesn't feel good, and even when we don't understand it. He wants what is best for us even more than we do.

Question(s):

If God told you that you would become ill, your spouse would leave you, you would lose your job, suffer unimaginable pain for years, but in the end, He would get the glory out of it, would you be eager to say, "Okay, God sign me up"? **Honestly, probably not!**

If God told you that you would chase wealth, women, and status, only to have it all taken away from you, leaving you to live a modest lifestyle but in the process, you would find Jesus, and He uses your life as a testimony of what true wealth is, would you happily walk away from the money, or would it be hard for you? Would you want to figure out a way to have all—the wealth, status, women, and Jesus? **A lot of men would say yes.**

If God told you that one day you would be ministering to women who suffered domestic and sexual abuse, but that this ministry was borne out of your own experiences, would you ask Him to spare you from this? **Probably so.**

If God told you that you would watch all your friends get married before you, but if you focused on Him, He would give you a special blessing, would you tell Him that you don't need the special blessing and just send your mate? What if He didn't do what you asked, would you go out and find one on your own? **Hmm…**

If God said to you, "I am going to give you a prophetic anointing…and I am going to give you a deliverance ministry that will save thousands, but you will suffer much, you will be neglected by your father as a child, you will feel unloved by your mother, you will suffer insecurities and self-hatred, the enemy will work untiringly to destroy your credibility and reputation, the spirit of Jezebel will attempt to follow you throughout your life because of the prophetic anointing and will try to launch many attacks against you," will you be first in line to sign up for this assignment? **Or would you say, "I think I will pass on this one Jesus"?**

God will often show us a glimpse of something. Maybe it is you preaching or standing before great men and women of God, maybe it is you ministering in other countries, maybe it is being married with children, owning your own business so that you can be a kingdom financier, or whatever the case. Most of the time, He doesn't tell us all the details of what it's going to take to get to the place He is showing us.

We must trust Him. His ways are not our ways, and His thoughts are not our thoughts. We must walk by faith. We like to know all the details upfront without having to labor for it. Truth is we need to constantly seek God for guidance. The quickest way to a God-given manifestation is God's way…period!

Submit to the process, whatever YOUR process is. Maybe it is just waiting and preparing. Maybe it is stepping out on faith and acting on what God told you to do even though you don't know how it's going to come to pass. Maybe your process is pressing and delving into deeper realms in God so that ministries can come forth. Maybe the process is you finally being honest with yourself and doing an exhaustive analysis on where you are in relation to where you should be, how you got there, and allowing God to get you back in line. Maybe your process is facing your giants (your flesh, fear, idiosyncrasies, people, etc.)

Wherever you find yourself in the process...just submit. You may not have understood that when you prayed for power with God, that meant that you would have to face some situations that almost made you want to give up. You didn't understand that you would have to deal with jealousy; you didn't know to get to the other side of manifestation, you had to walk through the valley of the shadow of death, and that you would go on a death walk to your flesh. You didn't know when you asked God to anoint you for deliverance that the stripes and precision of skill would come from your own war wounds. Nevertheless, it is necessary, and this is where you are. Do not die in the process. **Keep pressing; you've got a blessing waiting on you!**

It's for your good and for His glory. Whatever you must learn, whatever you have to develop, whatever you have to give up, whatever God is requiring from you in these situations...just do it. Submitting to the process simply means laying down your will and accepting and embracing God's will for your life. Submitting to God's will means to not fight against what He is trying to do in your life. It means complete acceptance and trust in the Author and Finisher of our faith and His ability to lead and navigate us through this journey. Submission looks like you, cooperating with the Holy Spirit in every way, and the process is simply the conduit in which this accomplishment is filtered through.

Just like the eagle that goes through the molting process, you might think you're dying in this stage because you feel weak, but you're not. Just feed yourself the Word of God, stay in His presence, and allow the older eagles that God sends you to impart, guide, and counsel you. Not only will you make it, but you will come out of the process stronger, wiser, more mature, more skilled than you were before. You will fly higher, you will go deeper, and you will be more effective and more powerful than ever.

Don't fight the process; buckle up and embrace it.

CHAPTER 4

Eat the Meat and Spit out the Bones

I remember my first introduction to this saying. A pastor I knew would always say eat the meat and spit out the bones, whether that be from a book you read, from a message you hear, or even a situation. There are times when we lack the ability to discern and the ability to decipher between truth and a lie, beneficial and detrimental, profitable and unprofitable, wise and unwise. We really have to be proactive as it relates to what we allow in our space, in our circle, in our minds, and in our hearts. The reason for this is because out of the abundance of the heart the mouth speaks, and out of our mouth are either curses or blessings. Because we have the spirit of God in us when our words part our mouth, they are infused with power... Now that power can be destructive or productive. What we put in our heart and in our spirit is what comes out. Sometimes there is a need to course correct or go on a spiritual detox when we have allowed pollutants to corrupt our thoughts and the meditation of our hearts. When this happens, it starts to show in our action, inaction, and decision-making.

What does "eat the meat and spit out the bones" really mean? It means to allow yourself to be nourished by the substance that is good, which is profitable and beneficial. Eat the part that will allow you to grow positively, eat the part that will allow you to mature, which will increase your capacity and ability to become your best self. To spit out the bones means that in getting to the meat...you may come across some bones—something that has no spiritual or natural nutritional value for you. It will not build you up; it will not help you mature. It doesn't mean it is always bad. It just may not be relevant to you. However, there are sometimes when those bones can cause destruction; it can warp your thinking and perception and can cause more damage than good. Therefore, it is always essential to edit everything you allow in your spirit through the Word of God, through what is true and right. And in order to know what that is, you must know not only the Word of God. You MUST KNOW HIM. There are a lot of people that know the Word of God and take it out of context, but when you know the writer of the Word... and you know His ways, His heart (as much as we can comprehend), then it helps in understanding the intent and revelation. It helps not to interpret His Word wrong when you have a relationship with He who IS the Word.

Information and knowledge are keys to growth. One of the ways in which we obtain knowledge is through books. Nowadays, you can choose to read a book or listen to it on things such as Audible or even YouTube. A good book can change the course of your life; it can awaken your soul, inspire you to achieve dreams; it can give you the blueprint to success and accomplishing goals. A good book can open a whole new world for you. And of course, there is no book that does this better than the Bible. Also, the Bible is the only book that can lay claim to be the infallible Word of God. While the Bible should always be a mainstay in our life and the book that guides us more than any other, God has anointed others to write books on various subjects that can help us along the way. Those books are intended to be an aid and resource in addition to the Bible…never in lieu of.

When the Bible was written, it was God-inspired…basically, God writing the book through the men He used. The Word of God has no error. It is all true. We must also admit the fact that this perfect and inerrant Word was translated by humans who may have made a few mistakes in interpretation or translation in some of the versions of the Bible, but the Word itself is true; and again, that is why it is always important to have a relationship with God intimately. While the truth of God's Word is indisputable, there are times where God may have anointed some of us to write books, and it genuinely is God-inspired and anointed, but because we are human, some of our own thoughts, ideologies, and perspectives may make it into the book, and that may be okay as long as we make the distinction between God's Word and our opinion or thoughts on a matter. It doesn't mean the opinion is right; it doesn't mean it is wrong; it just means it is the author's observation or opinion and should not be taken as Gospel. It is in times like this where this saying, "eat the meat, spit out the bones," comes into play.

For example, you may be reading a book by your favorite author, one who you genuinely believe to be a man or woman of God, and in their book, they may say it is okay to do something that you determined you would not do. Let's say it was always your belief that what they are endorsing was wrong, but hey…since your favorite preacher is now saying it is okay, you think to yourself, if they are doing it, and they are saved, then certainly you can, right? Well, you could…but why? You had already set a standard for yourself. Why would you relax that standard because you read something in a book by somebody you don't even really know? Just STOP and ask yourself, is this new bit of information you got profitable to you? Is it beneficial? Will it help you grow spiritually? Will it take you to a deeper place in God? Will it help you become the best version of yourself?

It is so easy to be swayed back and forth based on information…but we must learn how to be centered, unmovable, unswayable, even against our self if we are wrong. We must learn to leave ideas, opinions, people's way of doing things right where they are unless it BUILDS us up (in God). This is the time to show restraint and discipline; this is the time to lean into your principles. If you don't stand for something, you will fall for anything.

Books are a powerful tool and can make a world of difference; it can be a blessing…but we must be careful what we are putting into our spirit. We must be careful what we allow to shape our mind. So best practice would be to choose your books prayerfully. I may be a little extreme, but if I am looking for a book and I see one that interests me, I research the author. Now, that is if the book is for spiritual purposes. If I want a cookbook, I am not going to insist the person be apostolic because the purpose of the book is to get recipes. Point is, even in the best books—that are full of substance— even this book, you may find something that may be bones to you, and it may be meat for someone else. Guard your spirit, guard your anointing, and carefully choose what you read.

Likewise, with the music we listen to and the things we watch, the places we go, and the conversations that we have. Even in dealing with mentors or friends, take what is good.

All advice is not good advice, and not every good idea is a God idea. Take what is substance to you. Take what can build you up, what can help you, and properly progress you and spit out the bones. The greatest people in the world, people who I look up to, sometimes say things that are not right. It is their opinion. It does not make them bad; it makes them a human being with an opinion and their own way of thinking and doing things. Likewise, we must be careful not to push our opinion as if it is Gospel. We must clearly distinguish (especially for this millennial generation) where the Word of God starts and stops and where our opinions or suggestions begin. Accept what is right and leave anything else right where it is.

I think a lot of times we eat from who we like, and while I understand that…you must be careful that you don't eat things that you are not supposed to just because of your admiration for someone. On the other hand, if someone who you do not like says something that is true…you cannot deem it not true because you don't like them. No, truth is truth no matter who it comes from.

We must learn how to be centered in the truth. That will help us not to be swayed every which way. It will help us to eat the meat and spit out the bones no matter who is serving the meal. It will help us to always accept the truth and always reject error or wrong no matter who it comes from. Be centered in what is right. And what is right is what is in the Word of God.

Another example in which we really need to apply this thought of eating the meat and spitting out the bones is when it comes to messages over the pulpit. Unfortunately, depending on the preacher, you may get some messages that are not biblically sound at all. It is current events, topical messages, social issues, and opinions, all of which, I believe, are okay to preach and teach about as long as somehow and somewhere in the message the mind of God is being revealed, His principles, His direction, or His wisdom is being imparted. However, often...you can sit through a whole sermon and you get the opinion and the mind of man, not God. There is a place for opinions, but if it is delivered as if it is the Word of God, that is error. It needs to be clearly communicated that what is being given is the opinion of the speaker and not that of God. Even Apostle Paul did this in Scripture.

As preachers, teachers, leaders, saints, and servants, we have an obligation to be responsible with how we disseminate the Word of God. And as recipients, we are equally responsible to know the Word of God so that when we are on the receiving end, we know what to allow into our spirits and what to reject. We can't stay drinking milk forever. Eventually, we are expected to be able to eat the meat of the Word. Just because a preacher says it is okay to do something doesn't make it so. Just because they say something is not okay does not make it so. They are to give the Word of God, the mind of God... and when there is a departure, the responsible thing would be to let that be known so that the people can decide for themselves what they want to believe and receive. However, that decision should always be made based on the Word of God. As preachers, we are to proclaim and preach the Gospel, but we are not the writers of the Word. There may be times when the word that is delivered across the pulpit is not the word of God but the word of man, whether intentionally or unintentionally, and this is where your responsibility comes into play. It is then your job to eat the meat and spit out the bones, but you won't know which is which if you don't have His word hidden in your heart.

Know God, know His Word. Love Him enough that even if you are unsure of something, you err on the side of caution rather than risk until you get a clear answer from the LORD. And if you never get that clear answer from God Himself, His Word or a man or woman of God who gives a word that agrees with the Spirit of God in you and not your flesh, then keep on erring on the side of caution. Your soul is at stake.

The enemy would want to come in, right about now, and say to you, "This is too much," and that "God is not trying to keep you in bondage." Standards, rules, restraints, boundaries, and principles have a place in our walk with God, and when they are in line with His Word, they actually serve us well and feel more like safety than bondage to those whose hearts are pure. Satan has a way of twisting truths, just like he did in the garden with Eve. It is correct. God does not want you in any kind of bondage that will jeopardize your soul. But truth be told, you will be a prisoner to something or someone. You will either be a prisoner of the enemy, and hell will be your portion, or be a prisoner of Christ (the one who died for you), the one who will bless you for doing what is right and then reward you with eternal life. Paul talked about being a prisoner of the Lord in Ephesians chapter 4 and verse 1. You will serve one or the other; you choose. Me, personally, I'd rather be a prisoner to what is right than to what is wrong and destructive.

There is complete liberty and freedom in Christ and to those who have a clean heart and a pure spirit. Doing the right thing doesn't seem so dreadful unless our flesh is raging. The only time eating the meat and spitting out the bones is an issue is when our flesh desires those bones. It desires those things that are not good for us. Or the bones are more palatable to the appetite than the meat.

We don't want to become sick from food poisoning because of what we allow into our thoughts, our hearts, and our spirit. You are fully capable of making your own decisions. Jesus will not force you to do anything. But once you develop an intimate relationship with the LORD and you really get to know Him, you come to understand that He loves you more than you love yourself. He is not trying to punish you or keep you from having fun. Rather, He is trying to protect you from things that can harm you and cause destruction in ways you can't even grasp. Letting the wrong thing in your spirit will allow a seed to be planted that will sprout up at an inopportune time and throw you off course. So be mindful, be watchful, and guard your spirit. Stand on the principles of God.

Filter and choose carefully what you watch, who you hang with, the conversations you have, where you go, who and what you receive from, and what you allow into your space until holiness, truth, and light are innate in you—even then you still have to be careful. After all, you are guarding something invaluable. And that is the Spirit of God that lives on the inside of you, and not only that. There is a purpose, there are gifts and talents that lay on the inside of you, waiting to be manifested. You are a treasure, so treat yourself as such. You will attract what you are.

You must learn to feed your spirit what is true and guard against the junk that will kill your spirit or distract you and take you off course. Meat will feed your spirit; bones will feed your flesh or either take up room so that you are full but have been fed a meal with no nutritional value, thus operating on empty calories and receiving no spiritual nourishment. Meat is any and everything that lines up with the Word of God, any and everything that builds you up naturally and or spiritually to be the man or woman of God that He has called you to be. Anything else is dung.

The more you feed your spirit, the more you starve your flesh. The more you feed your flesh or neglect to feed your spirit, the more you starve your spirit. Eat the things that will be of spiritual nutritional value to you. Filter what you allow into your mind, heart, and spirit.

Eat the meat and spit out the bones in every area of your life!

CHAPTER 5

Pedestals

I remember when I first start going to church. I was so awestruck by the saints. Here I was, raw and rough around the edges... I had been through more at twenty years old than some people had been through in a lifetime. Prior to salvation, being around gangsters and drug dealers were a norm for me. I saw a lot, experienced a lot, but trying to fit in and adapt to a totally different culture was new and very disconcerting. The disparity in my mind between myself and the saints, especially leaders, was great. I wasn't sure if I could measure up; they seemed so untarnished and pure.

Over time, my eyes were opened to a more balanced reality. I remember an experience where I put someone on a pedestal. In short, they were anointed, and I deeply admired them. It started off like any other mentor-and-mentee relationship. And like some of the others, we also ended up becoming friends. I didn't know that at the time, behind the scenes, this person was going through one of the most horrific and diabolical situations imaginable. To me, they were a spiritual giant. They had an "S" on their chest, and they were a demon slayer. However, behind the scenes, I was witnessing firsthand my spiritual superhero—afraid, and backing down against the enemy. What they needed was someone to get in the fight with them and cover them…and I did, but not without voicing my disappointment.

See, they were messing up my view of them. I had put them on this pedestal. I had expectations of how they would deal with the enemy if ever confronted in a fight like they were in. I could not believe that this person who had the power to snatch people out of hell with their preaching when they were under the anointing was the same person who feared this spirit of Jezebel and Leviathan that was coming after them when they were left to themselves. See, I was a fighter… I grew up fighting, so I could not understand why this mentor wouldn't fight for themselves.

The details of this story are inconsequential. What is relevant is the fact that I saw their humanity in this situation. I saw the flaws, and before I was able to really look through the lens of compassion and mercy, I was very disappointed on many levels. Sometimes, even the people that we think are the strongest, most anointed, most pure, toughest, wisest, and most spiritual may show us something contrary to what we have come to expect from them. It happens; they are human and so are you. There are times when someone put unrealistic expectations on you and got disappointed because you were unable to fulfill them. God doesn't tell us to put our expectation of perfection off on others.

To be honest, I can admit that I bordered on making this person an idol in my life. They could do no wrong, and some of the time that I would spend with God, I started giving to this friendship. I tell you what: God does not play. He is a jealous God, and He wants to be the only one to sit on the throne of your heart. There is nothing wrong with admiring people, but when you do it in a way that gives them God's glory (whether you realize it or not), you are putting them and yourself in a dangerous situation. So best practice is to honor the God in people and give mercy and compassion to the human, but never give them what belongs to God. Only Jesus is perfect, and expecting anyone else to be is unfair and borders on hypocritical if we don't hold our own selves to that same standard. Even if we do, we still aren't perfect, and we have no right to demand that from others. Putting others on pedestals is a surefire way to experience disappointment. Every time. If someone puts you on a pedestal, they will experience disappointment. God will allow us to be knocked off our high horse, especially if you allowed someone to put you on it.

Sometimes the expectations we put on others may cause them to feel obligated to measure up. This is unwise. An expectation leaves little room for deviation because we have in our mind already the outcome of that expectation. And while you cannot control what another person does, we should be protectors of our brothers and sisters and love them with knowledge and wisdom. Meaning, you don't pressure them to perform or make them feel as if they must wear an "S" on their chest, which in turn may cause them to wear masks or project an image just to fulfill your expectations of them. Rather, love and wisdom would cause us to challenge them to greatness but not set them up for failure. Challenging or encouraging someone else should be about them, and not about you. Expectation is about you and you alone. See, some of these same people that I put on pedestals are people that I would have done anything for, I would go to the ends of the earth to support or lend a hand to. But when I needed something and couldn't find the help or support I desired… I cannot lie and say thoughts of resentment didn't try to take over and set in. Here I was giving my all, and it seemed as if people did not appreciate it. Here I was singing the praises of people I put on pedestals, and when they did not respond the way I thought they should respond when I needed something, I was hurt and disappointed. I expected that they would be to me what I was to them. I expected that they had the capacity to give to me what I thought I was giving to them.

However, I had to ask myself a tough question: Did God tell me to do all those things to begin with? Matter of fact, sometimes the people I felt let me down never asked me to do half of the things that I did. Here I was expecting them to pay me back or show me some sort of appreciation for something that they did not ask for and that I had willingly done. Also, sometimes we don't realize, we want appreciation to be shown back to us the way we want it, but maybe someone did show you appreciation in the way that they knew to give it, but because it wasn't what you were looking for, you missed it. See, all of this can get convoluted, and this is how you would know God is not in it. He is not the Author of confusion.

Sometimes we need to course-correct. We need to be pure in spirit and clean in our heart. It does not profit us to put unrealistic expectations on people. And it is unrealistic expectations deriving from wrong motives and faulty thinking. Truth is, oftentimes no one is asking us to put them on a pedestal. It is our own doing that causes us to overextend. God is not requiring you to go above and beyond to show someone how highly you have exalted them in your world, and He definitely is not requiring that in turn, they show you appreciation or payment for something that is ungodly in the first place. Putting people on pedestals has nothing to do with

God and everything to do with our own thinking and imma-
turity. And I think therein lies the issue. It is "our" thinking
that messes us up every time. We need to be transformed by
the renewing of our minds that we may be able to discern
what is good, pleasing, and the perfect will of God (not our
will). However, often, we end up trying to discern out of our
finite and limited mind instead of the mind of God.

So when you put people on pedestals, when you give of
yourself in ways God has not required, it ceases to be about
God, and it becomes about you. When things are not recip-
rocated as you think they should be, then resentment and
bitterness kick in because you were not doing things out of
the pureness of your heart to begin with. You were operating
out of your faulty heart. And it is out of a faulty heart that
causes us to put expectations on people that God did not put
on them. Sooner or later, if you ever find yourself in a place
where you put a person, place, or thing higher than it ought
to have been…a lesson is coming, and that lesson is: DO NOT
PUT PEOPLE ON PEDESTALS…ONLY JESUS BELONGS THERE.

Almost everyone in this walk has put more confidence
in a person than they should have and, as a result, has had
to learn a very valuable lesson, which is: it is better to put
your trust in God than in man. When we put people on the
pedestal that only God belongs on, it usually ends up in disappointment. Sometimes our admiration is displaced, and
we make idols out of those we look up to. Instead of admiring the giver of the gift, we worship the gift and the person who God is using. Often, we do not grasp the gravity of
our actions and how powerful they can be. It is important to
note that the people we put undue confidence in are flawed
human beings just like we are. They just have a grace and an
anointing given by God that is to be used for His purpose

and His glory. Now, the wisest vessels will give any praise and glory given to them right back to God. The wisest and most learned saints will resist the temptation to perform to gain your praise and admiration. But honestly, even the most seasoned of ministers have fallen prey to the temptation to cloak themselves with the adoration and glory that only belongs to the Lord, and some even seek it. There are men and women of God who are used greatly, and they are battling with pride (anyone who is anointed must battle this spirit), and they are well-meaning, but sometimes they desire validation and/or praise. Again, this is something any anointed person must fight, so let's not make it harder for them and lavish them with delusions of grandeur.

Ask yourself, what is your motive?

Are you complimenting them to feed into an insecurity that you see so that you can get in good with them? Is it an ill-informed attempt to encourage and build them up? Most people want to be where they are celebrated, but a wise person prefers a place where they can get the truth in love. There is nothing wrong with admiring a person; there is nothing wrong with complimenting someone. However, admire them, but don't worship them. You would do better to admire the God in them and to let that be known. Be wise with your words; give compliments that point back to God, especially if God gives you the insight to see that this person may struggle with confidence (as anointed as they are) or enjoy or need your validation a little too much. You want them to continually seek God, not seek you for your compliments. Genuine love doesn't set people up for failure. If you really admire a person, and if you really love them, get them off that pedestal, quit tempting them to perform, and challenge them to find glory in God.

You are not doing anyone any favors by over-complimenting and treating people like they are your God. Matter of fact, you are putting yourself and them in a dangerous position. God is a jealous God. He doesn't want us to have any other gods before Him, and if you are treating someone as such and they are not quick to reject what you are doing and they are flirting with taking a seat on that pedestal you are building for them, then they are in grave danger as well.

The best advice that I could give is to be led by God. Have a reason for what you are doing, and let that reason be rooted in love, truth, wisdom, and not manipulation, wrong motive, or ungodly strategy. We must take better care of each other. No, you can't control what another person does, but if we have any amount of discernment at all, we can see pride, we can see insecurity, we can sense when people need our validation. And if it is God leading you to give validation, then fine, but if it's not, we cause more harm than good.

There is a proper way to exhort, encourage, and build up. If it is God, you can do it as much as your heart desires. There is nothing wrong with reinforcing the truth again and again. Matter of fact, it is necessary to combat all the negativity that the enemy tries to tell us. So if God uses you to impart strength and confidence in someone, that is good. That is the Bible. We want to build people up in God. We want to encourage the God in them, not their flesh. We want to remind one another of who we are in God. We want to remind people of the strength, grace, and ability possible to them through Christ Jesus. Putting your confidence in a man or putting someone on a pedestal glorifies man, but we want to glorify God. The people that we sometimes put on pedestals are humans who make mistakes, and if they feel as if they are not allowed the room to do so, I have seen where this has led to grave outcomes. These people that we look up to are as supernatural as you are and are as human as you are. They are not made from steel. The person on that pedestal struggles just like you do; they are trying to figure it out just like you are. It would do good for us to remember that.

There were several incidents that opened my eyes to the fact that everyone in the church is a human being and doesn't always have on their Superman cape or Wonder Woman outfit while slaying and fighting demons. A lot of us are wiping tears with one hand and slashing the darts of the enemy with the other hand. Now that is not to say treat the man or woman of God like they are common or familiar or regard them with no respect and honor. That is far from what I am saying. It took me years to get a balanced view of this thing. The people that God has anointed have a grace and an ability to do the work of the LORD; it doesn't make them perfect. What we must learn is that it is imperfect people that God is using. That is a part of what makes it so powerful. This is what brings glory to God: The fact that He can take someone borne into sin and shaped into iniquity and birth them again into His kingdom and use them for His glory.

Let's be mindful and start taking people down from pedestals. You can still honor them and respect them, even regard them highly. But don't put them on a pedestal. They are humans with real problems and emotions of their own just like you. They are working out their soul salvation with fear and trembling just like you are. They can make mistakes, and we still must learn how to respect and honor them IF they are a man or woman of God. And we do not get to decide who is a man or woman of God; that is His job. If we have shouted the praises of people or our leaders and then they make a mistake (not talking about them sinning or living in sin), or they do something that we disagree with, it speaks to your maturity when that changes the way you see them. I am so glad that we can make mistakes and God doesn't change who we are or see us differently.

Now think about this: how do you handle being disappointed by a leader? What if they do something that you think is wrong, or they make a decision that you disagree with? Can you still honor, respect, obey, and submit to leadership when you have been hurt, let down, seemingly looked over, or rejected? Maybe they are following the directive of the Lord, and you either are not mature enough to understand, or it simply is not your business and you have no need to understand. Also, you may have needed to experience a situation that would cause you to take that leader off that pedestal because it truly is detrimental in every way.

Again, nobody belongs on a pedestal but God, but the leader that God placed you under should still be shown honor and respect, regardless of any disagreement, hurt, or otherwise. Even if, in fact, they made a mistake, this is the time to consider yourself as you consider them. Give them grace as you would want it. There should never be anything that someone does, no matter who they are, that can get us out of the will of God. Mistake or not, disappointment or not, if God planted you somewhere, you don't pick up and go because someone let you down, or even hurt you unless God tells you to. We don't make decisions out of our emotions. You move when God says move, and if He doesn't tell you to, then you stay. Now, I am not talking about leaders making egregious mistakes or living in sin. No, we call that what it is, and we only follow the leader as they follow God. However, I am talking about when the person who we feel let us down is a man or woman living a holy lifestyle. Leaders will make mistakes. We should require them to stop making mistakes the day that we stop.

Often we run instead of facing situations and walking them out, and that is why we constantly go through the same things no matter where we are. The leader is not your God. Don't expect perfection from them. Expect them to seek God with all their heart and might, but when they make a mistake, allow grace and mercy. Same as you would want someone to do with you. Don't put unrealistic expectations on the men and women of God and set yourself up to be hurt. They are not called to replace our natural fathers and mothers. They are not called to even be our friend or come to all our engagements. Leaders are not called to hang out with you nor to be accessible to you at any given time. So we might as well tear down those expectations right now. If they are your pastor, they are called to watch for your souls. If they are your leader in a ministry, they are called to challenge, cultivate, and inspire you through instruction and teaching on how to fulfill the mandate or objective of that ministry. We must stop looking for people to try and make up for what we have lacked.

If we honor them, and if we admire them, wouldn't that same honor remain in the presence of a situation that doesn't go in our favor? It shouldn't diminish because our expectation was not fulfilled. See, what we do is pour empty honor, praise, and over-the-top gestures at the people that we seemingly respect or admire, but let them disagree with us, let them rebuke us, let them not handle us like we think we should be handled, then some of us now curse the same people we used to bless. What happened to the pedestal that we placed them on? Did they only deserve what "we called" honor when they did everything according to the way we thought they should do it? Something is very wrong with this thinking. What happens is that we look up to people and make super heroes out of them, and then when in their humanness they make a mistake or do something that we don't agree with, now we're hurt, disappointed, broken, and confused and ready to leave the church or ready to retreat because we put someone on a pedestal that we shouldn't have (never mind if what they did was right or not [because it could be that your thinking is wrong in the situation... Lord forbid]), but even if they were legitimately wrong, do they not get the same grace and room to grow as God has given you?

What happens if your leader doesn't think you are ready for an assignment or something that you want to do? Are they now not worthy of honor and submission? See, the thing about pedestals is if YOU put someone on the pedestal, then you can take them off.

Some of us not only put other leaders on pedestals, but we put our counterparts on pedestals, people we feel have gifts and or talents that we may not possess. Truth is, we all have something special that God blessed us with. We just need to get our eyes off everybody else and on Jesus so that He can help us to know who He created us to be. When we build that intimate relationship with Jesus, when we have confidence in the relationship that we have with Him, we will cease to put people on pedestals because we come to understand that only He belongs there. Only Jesus is qualified to sit on a throne. Only He is faultless, and only He is worthy. In all things, balance is key. Give honor, give respect, allow room for people to be human and to grow in grace, exercise mercy and compassion. Don't put anyone on a pedestal and don't think more highly of yourself than you ought to. We all are trying to make it. Whether you are an apostle or a lay member in the church, all of us have come short of the glory of God. Yet all of us should be striving to be as much like Jesus as we can be.

CHAPTER 6

Being Delivered from People

I've heard people say several times that they need to be "delivered from people." This saying is not suggesting that one become a recluse and live on their own island—just the opposite. Rather, I believe the thought is that we would gain victory in overcoming the effect of people's opinions and actions toward us. The brilliance in God's design of relationships is that it serves as a vessel or carrier if you will. The relationships we have allow things to be conveyed, transported, and delivered through us to another. Through relationships; ideas, attitudes, behaviors, and emotions are transmitted from one person to the other. Ideally, we can be used as an extension of Jesus to connect and plug into others as He moves in us to get to those that may need His love, comfort, support, healing, wisdom, kindness, gentleness, power, understanding, or touch. In a perfect world, the Lord would be able to move through us freely with no hindrances or restrictions. However, this all too often is not the case.

We have been born into sin and shaped in iniquity. We were born in a fallen world. With this in mind, we understand that everyone has traveled a road unique to them with their own experiences that they have processed in their own way. When we encounter each other, most of the times we have no clue what the other person has had to go through in their life, and how it has shaped them. **Our eyes have fallen on a lot of people, but how many of those people have we truly seen?** Truth is we very rarely "see" them. We see what is presented, and that is our excuse. Sometimes we think that this somehow absolves us of the responsibility of really caring and really getting to know one another. It is easy to engage those with whom you feel are like you, but what about those that you feel are different? I'm referring to the people you don't understand or those that might make you feel uncomfortable for one reason or the other. Maybe it is them, or maybe it is you. **What work do you do to bridge the divide, or does it remain?** If we decide who we will and will not engage with, we cease to allow God to move as freely as He would like.

If we could pick the people that our world consisted of, or the people we had to deal with daily, a lot of us would choose people that were like us. We would choose friends and family with similar mindsets. We would choose those who we liked and who were easy to get along with. We would select those that we believed thought the way we do. And for those of us who feel as if we are a little smarter than the norm, we may choose a diverse group of people—people that would challenge us—but only so far. We certainly would not pick people that would hurt us, betray us, use us, abuse, reject us, try to destroy us, and so on. We probably wouldn't even want people around us with mindsets that were the total opposite of ours, especially if it were to take us out of our comfort zone.

This is where I reiterate the brilliance of Jesus. Saved or not, we really do not get to pick the people we encounter. We don't control the people that we meet on our jobs, in our families, in our churches, social outreaches, school, in the store, while on vacation, etc. As a result, engaging with people who may not be our cup of tea can put us in positions that may make us uncomfortable. This can be good for us. It teaches us how to interact with others that we would not normally give the time of day. We are put in positions that cause us to stretch, to adjust, to learn, to grow, and to consistently evolve. If we are only around people who think like us and never challenge our emotions, beliefs, thoughts, ways, and so on, I can't see how we would be able to grow past where we are.

However, if we are challenged in some way or exposed to new information or a different perspective or experiences, it can stretch us. It can increase our capacity to evolve. If I never suffer at the hands of someone who has done me wrong, and I never experience pain or dismay, then my growth is stunted, and my compassion and scope are limited. There is a benefit to having relationships and experiences that cause friction. Friction has its disadvantages, but it also has its advantages. Friction can cause fire, and as this relates to us, the friction in interactions, misunderstanding, trials, and so on with people can create a fire that is meant to burn out everything in us that is not like God. It allows impurities to rise to the top so that they can be revealed, and we can deal with them. God does all things well. He has a reason for everything He allows, and even when it does not feel good, if we love Him, it is for our good. It is with this thought that I proceed into the topic of "being delivered from people."

God created relationships. It is His desire that we fellowship with one another. It is His desire that we connect with one another that we may learn, draw strength, encourage, support, love, build up, and work with one another in a shared goal. It is with loving kindness that God draws us. He also wants to work with us by using us as an extension of Himself and showing His loving kindness so that He may draw others to Himself through us. Remember, we are to be a carrier, a vessel; we are a medium of transport and transmission. We are transmitting the love of God and His Word.

To embrace getting to know others is to embrace growth and all that it entails. I am not saying let any and every one into your intimate circle of friends. Nor am I saying throw common sense and discernment out the window. More so, I am saying, be open to the people that God put in your path, and before you reject or dismiss them, ask if they are there for a reason. We don't have to be best friends with people to show them the love of God, to support them, or build them up. And it doesn't make us enemies if we have disagreements or if we have hurt one other. We are flawed human beings, and while that is not an excuse, it is a reason. We can go through things that make us feel like we want to do away with people altogether, but we are not an island. We need one another, no matter how flawed and broken we may be. **We still need each other, and building a prison to keep others out only causes us to be locked in.**

Isolation is a dangerous place, and it is the devil's playground. So understand, he will do whatever he can to get you to that place. Submit to God, resist the devil, and he shall flee. We are to acknowledge God in all our ways so that He may direct our path, and that includes how we deal with people and how we internalize and process how they deal with us. Resist the desire to stay a victim; resist the desire to allow the words and actions of others to dictate how you feel about yourself; resist allowing your emotions to cause you to make grave mistakes. Resist being controlled by your flesh, and allow your spirit to lead you in all truth and in all things. And if we do this, then the devil will have to flee; he will not have a leg to stand on. We will have left no doors opened and no windows cracked for him to sneak in.

The enemy is strategic. One of the things that he does is manipulate vulnerable and carnal vessels. Often, these are people that are either not spiritually mature or people that are broken or offended. The devil hates anything good. Anything that God has purposed to use for His glory, the enemy will try and destroy, and that includes your relationships or associations with people. Now there are times when it is appropriate to completely disconnect from a person and pray for them. If a person has been sent by the enemy to kill your spirit, you may want to put some distance between you and them until God gives you clear direction. However, on the flip side, there are those people that afflict our flesh, and we are ready to do away with them. It is necessary to have people in our life that cause us friction in areas that we need to work on anyway. Just because a person is causing you discomfort and pain doesn't mean that it is the enemy. It could be God, especially if it is causing you to have to die to your flesh and let love reign. If it is causing you to kill pride or look inwardly or be patient or more understanding, more compassionate, kinder, stronger, etc., then it may just be God. He uses these things to make us better. We are so busy trying to cut people out of our life when God is trying to help us grow and learn how to develop meaningful relationships with people that we would not normally choose on our own, even if the purpose is just for ministry or business. God allows people that challenge us in some sort of way to strengthen our character and purify our spirit, especially if they are challenging us to love more like Jesus.

For all intents and purposes of this chapter, I am not talking about allowing relationships in your life with people that are serving the enemy. If what a person is saying to you or is doing to you does not align with God's will for your life, if a person is tearing you down, setting snares, trying to assassinate you spiritually by attacking your assignment… your identity…or your integrity, then those are people that should be dealt with spiritually (because the weapons of our warfare are not carnal but mighty through God), but by all means, I am not saying try to cultivate a relationship with them. Pray for them and release them until or unless God instructs otherwise. We never want to throw the baby out with the bathwater, and just maybe someone as described above can be delivered, but I don't believe God would use you to try and deliver another person's soul if it will put yours at stake. Not so. There is only one God, and His name is Jesus, so you don't have to play savior to anyone at the expense of your salvation. God does not require that of us. So anyone in your life that puts your soul in jeopardy, disconnect from them immediately.

Now, on the other hand, there are some people that will challenge your patience and anything else that you believe yourself to be, and just because this person is difficult to deal with (to you) or challenges you in ways that others won't doesn't mean that they are of the devil. Matter of fact, they may just be rubbing you the wrong way because dealing with them highlights inadequacy or inefficiency in your approach or in your relation to God's people (all of his people, however different they may be). It may be revealing a weakness that we need to work on; it may be uprooting a flaw. This type of challenge is good. But often, this is the type of challenge that we run from. We are uncomfortable dealing with someone that requires us to come more outside of ourselves to embody the attributes of Christ in order to understand, relate, and be able to fully receive the benefit of experiencing people that are different than you, who, in your encounter with them, may cause you to grow in ways you didn't even know you needed.

This world is filled with all different types of people that come from different backgrounds, people who have experienced various things and processed those things in various ways depending upon their capacity, surroundings, culture, atmosphere, home life, teachings, and the way they think. It is impossible to understand people fully and completely; that is reserved for God alone. Only Jesus is all-knowing. It is impossible to try to make sense out of things that sometimes make no sense. It is nerve-racking and peace disturbing to try and interpret every action of human beings. That is NOT our job. If we have a right relationship with God, He will give us all the information we need. He will give knowledge, discernment, wisdom, and information when necessary. He will make us aware of what we need to know when we need to know it...and for some, insight is just innate. So if you allow God's Spirit to lead in everything you do and allow His love to be central in every action you make, then that will help tremendously. Trying to assess people and things with our finite and limited understanding will render a flawed and half-baked conclusion every time. Trying to understand the intents of man's heart with our natural mind is dangerous, beyond our capacity, and completely tiresome. Believe me,

I know. I have one of the most analytical minds I've ever come across, and if we are not careful, what God designed to be a strength can become a weakness if we don't know its purpose and how to use and manage that strength. I found myself trying to understand and make sense out of everything a person said, everything that they did, and because I feel very deeply—and in ways I cannot even verbalize—I was left frustrated and confused when I was unable to make sense out of things that were very illogical and born out of chaos, disorder, insecurity, hatred, and pain.

When we experience persecution, affliction, tribulation, famine, and hardship, and we evaluate and draw our own conclusion that there was nothing we did to bring about this trouble, we often feel as if what we are going through is unjustified. However, we are accounted as sheep for the slaughter all day long. The Bible says, "For our light affliction, which is but for a moment, works for us a far more exceeding eternal weight of glory." (2 Corinthians 4:17). The Bible also says, "For I reckon that the sufferings of this present time are not worthy to be compared with the glory which shall be revealed in us" Romans 8:18. RIGHT UP THROUGH HERE IS WHERE WE MISS IT.

Our perception is off; we might be right about what happened but wrong in regard to why it happened or why it was allowed. We don't have proper insight, so a lot of times, we make the wrong decisions and respond to things the wrong way because we have no clue what is really going on in the spiritual realm or in a much broader view. We might have facts but no understanding. I once heard a preacher say, "A little information would make cooperation a WHOLE LOT EASIER." Sometimes if we just understood why we were going through something, it would make the process less challenging. But what about when you don't have information or an understanding? What do you do when you feel as if you are being done wrong and you really have no clue why? BEFORE YOU ACT, **talk to God.**

Often, it is when we lack understanding or insight that causes us to act out of emotion. Sometimes God wants to show us where we are. It's easy to obey when you understand. It is easy to submit or accept rebuke when you know that you are guilty. But what about when "you" feel as if the treatment is unwarranted? Do you have the right to act on your own? Do you have the right to set people straight, to put them in their place? Do you have the right to fight your own battle, thus removing the need for God to fight it for you? God forbids. See, sometimes, God not only allows these things…but He orchestrates them. **So be careful that you are not fighting against people that are carrying out the will of God, which inevitably is meant to make you, build you up, or develop you in some area,** especially when it has to do with a godly leader.

God may be testing you for promotion. He may be setting you up for elevation based upon your response in the situation. God may be allowing that leader to be hard on you to see if they can trust your character, your integrity, to see if you will fight in your flesh or submit to the Holy Ghost in you. Of course, God already knows what you will do, but sometimes we don't realize where we really are in God as it relates to our maturity, submission, and integrity…so we need reality checks.

Often, leaders do things to test (not tempt) you. They are not God; they are not all-knowing; however, if the right character exists within us, then whatever the leader does to test us would result in the right response anyway, right? So if we respond in a way that reveals something that we may need to work on, that is still a positive to us because now we are aware and can do something about it. **Perspective is everything.**

When I was sent to my current church and started experiencing things from people that I knew where real men and women of God, it perplexed me. I almost had a mental breakdown because I could not discern at the time what God was doing in this situation. I would go over and over my actions, what I said versus what the person had said or done and could find no fault, yet the way they were dealing with me didn't line up with my conclusion. It threw me off because I didn't understand what God was doing. I often felt the need to fight my own battles when I knew they were wrong. Thing is…it wasn't about who was right or wrong; they were not sinning; they may not have even known why they were treating me the way they were or maybe they did. Point is…they were a vessel; God was using them to show me I was not ready for where He was taking me.

What God was trying to do was get that need to set people straight when they were wrong out of me, that need to buck up against what I felt was wrong. God is supposed to fight the battles, not me. The only battles I am to engage in are the ones in the spirit that are sanctioned by God, not the ones in my flesh. See, I would submit if I agreed, but if I felt that what you were doing was wrong, then that is when I would have a problem, and that is exactly what God was trying to get out of me. He was teaching me to submit even when I didn't understand. He wanted me to submit even when I felt like people were treating me like dirt. He did not want me to fight for myself. In no way am I saying God wanted me to submit to a leader that was unrighteous or committing a sin—that is something altogether different. I am talking about true men and women of God. So He allowed situations constantly that put me in a predicament that would challenge my way of looking at things; it would challenge how I thought things should be done, and over and over, I kept going in circles and ending up back in the same place. I could not forgo the process of learning this crucial principle. The principle was OBEDIENCE, whether you like it or not. The principle was be faithful, whether you like the conditions or not.

The thing is, I considered myself to be deeply moral and insightful. For me, the principle mattered. What was right mattered. But what if what I thought was right was actually wrong? See, I did not factor that into the equation because arrogance assumed that my way of thinking about things was always right. A lot of people are stuck right here. You may be in denial, but this is you all day long. In my case, I thought, because of the encounters I had with God, and the way He talked to me, and the way He dealt with me, it put me in a whole other level of understanding, which may have been true, but it wasn't exclusive to myself alone. I had allowed haughtiness to prevail. True intimacy with God in its purest form should cultivate compassion, humility, love, and passion…not self-righteousness! Those of us who are leaders would do well to remember this.

Who determines right or wrong? If I being a woman of God take a position on a matter that is contrary to the position that a leader, who is a man or woman of God takes, who is right and who is wrong, and who gets to decide? What if both can back it up with a scripture? Then what? This is for another chapter in another book, but for the purposes of this example in this chapter, the answer would be: the leader gets to decide. Who can decide that a course of action is wrong or right if it is not clearly spelled out in Scripture literally? If it's not a matter of allowing or promoting sin, but just a matter of how people think a situation should be handled? I would say the leader of the church or the leader of the ministry has the power to make the decision. Many will not agree, and this is not always the answer…but all things being right and above board, then my answer remains the same. See, this is where trust and submission come into play. If I trusted a leader enough to become a part of the ministry that they are leading, then I should trust them and submit to their decision-making, even when it is contrary to what I would have decided. They are the leader, not me. Again, not talking about things clearly spelled out in Scripture, or corrupt leaders. I am talking about leaders that are righteous and doing the best they can as the Lord leads them. This is what I had to learn, to not challenge everything when I didn't agree. I had to learn to pick and choose my battles. I had to also learn that I was not always right.

For example, what if you challenged or bucked up against what a leader had done because you were totally convinced that it was the wrong thing, seemed apparent that your reasoning was correct, and even got other people to believe the same thing, only to find out after the fact—from the Lord no less—that you were wrong. Do we understand the damage that can be caused from our actions? Do you now go back to all the people that you damaged and make it right? Do you apologize? Or do you accept correction in secret without informing others of the truth?

See, God could not trust me to be committed and faithful to the call He placed on my life if when I disagreed or was challenged in some way, I would retreat or either try to settle the matter myself. That is unwise and immature. I know I am not the only one that has found themselves in this situation. God allows these things to happen because He is processing you. He is making you, developing you, strengthening your resiliency, fortifying your bounce back, cultivating and working extreme obedience and submission in you so that He can trust you with what He put in you.

So we get in the church and have run-ins with people, misunderstandings, suffer persecution and affliction, and we look at the people by whom the offense or act comes, not understanding God is allowing it to work something out of you and to work something in you. We hold grudges with people for years, looking at them sideways, unable to work in ministry with them because we could not discern the lesson in the situation. Maybe God constantly gave you difficult people to work with you so He could develop your ability to work with all types of personalities and still be productive. Maybe, you are someone He will use to see gifts in others, and He will use you to bring it out…well, that is an arduous process, and if you can't deal with difficult people who supposedly know who they are in God, how will you be able to handle those who don't know who they are yet?

God's ways are not our ways, and His thoughts are not our thoughts. His ways are past finding out. God needs willing vessels that are pliable to His will. He needs to be able to bend us in any which way He needs when He needs it. And if there are strongholds or roots of stubbornness, or rebellion in us for whatever reason…it needs to go. So the chipping away at those fortresses begins, and that is often done through situations that occur with people. We talk about being delivered from people when really, what we need is understanding and to be delivered from our thinking. Do you realize that when people hate on you, talk about you, or even try to set snares for you, if God is allowing that, then there is a lesson in it for you? It is for you to gain some sort of knowledge, wisdom, strength, resiliency, or victory.

I've often heard people say that they have to be delivered from people. What does that really mean anyway—be delivered from PEOPLE? I would venture to say what we really need to be delivered from in most cases is "ourselves" and how we perceive and how we respond to certain things.

It is the step-by-step, the applicable instructions on "how to be delivered" that often escape us. And while the answer is in several scriptures, sometimes it must be broken down to us in layman's terms. Sometimes deliverance is instantaneous and can come through us praying for ourselves, someone praying for us, laying hands on us, receiving a word from the Lord, etc. Other times, deliverance can be a process in which certain steps must be carried out or must occur. A lot of times, while these steps are being carried out, a new level of knowledge and/or revelation is taking place. Transforming of the mind is happening; an awakening, enlightening, and insight is being imparted through this experience that can make the deliverance that much more memorable. These are the kind of deliverances where we learn lessons, and God uses that because now that we are delivered, we can then go back and walk somebody else through their situation from inception through to deliverance. You can give insight that you may not have been able to give if your deliverance wasn't through a process. It doesn't mean you know exactly how they feel, or that you went through the exact same scenario, but at its root, the path to deliverance is the same.

Now to bring this all together.

Being delivered from people really means to be delivered from yourself! It really means to learn how to manage your emotions. How to appropriately feel and process what is happening and filter your response or nonresponse through the Holy Spirit and allow God to lead you on how to proceed. Not every action deserves a reaction from us. I would say most times it is not about the other person at all. We must learn how to develop thick spiritual skin and let things roll off so that we remain centered in God and unaffected. We need to learn how to guard our hearts. Part of that starts with what we allow into our spirit...and what we allow in our spirit is often the things that we have allowed in our thoughts and meditated on.

One of my favorite scriptures is Philippians 4:8 which says, "Whatsoever things are true, whatsoever things are honest, whatsoever things are just, whatsoever things are pure, whatsoever things are lovely, whatsoever things are of good report, if there be any virtue, and if there be any praise, think on these things." This scripture arms you with one of the tactics of warfare.

When a person, the enemy, or even yourself tries to tell you something that is contrary to what God says about you, you must learn to reject what is said; don't meditate on it or rehearse it in your mind over and over. No! Instead, immediately reject that untruth or that attack and replace that thought with what is true. Rehearse what is good, what is honest, what is pure; think on those things. This is a part of the "how-to" in being delivered. Ask God to give clarity on what is happening, why it is happening, and ask Him what you are supposed to learn in the situation or what you are supposed to do in the situation.

In some of these situations where you feel as if you are being attacked or unfairly treated, you are not discerning your role in the situation correctly. Sometimes we are playing victim to the aggressor when God is allowing this thing to take place because He wants YOU to stand up and help deliver the person that you feel is wronging you. It is all about perspective. But perspective alone is not enough…what you need is a word from God. What we need is keen discernment, we need to be able to accurately understand what is taking place, and that is only done through relationship and communication with God.

God sits high and looks low. He alone has the full view of the ripple effects of one action or inaction. He alone fully understands why He allows things to happen and why He prevents other things. It will save us from a whole lot of mental weariness and stress if we learn early on to let God be God and just trust in His sovereignty. Trying to do God's job will drive you insane and stress you out to the point that it can make you physically sick. LEAVE God's BUSINESS ALONE. Learn your part; stay in the lane God put you in. We must understand this to even begin the journey of being delivered from people (ourselves).

It is true that "hurt people hurt people." Everyone gets hurt from time to time. That is inevitable. However, there is an issue if one refuses to heal from the hurt. It is when we get stuck in the hurt and cannot move past it because we feel as if we have a right to be offended that becomes the problem. Being unable to move on from an offense is a good indicator that pride may be lurking. It is pride because what we are saying is "How could they do this to me" as if we are of higher stature than Jesus Himself. Maybe you feel like you have been good to the person that hurt you, or you feel as if you have sacrificed for them, or you feel like you have not done anything to them to deserve the hurt that you received, so you take the hurt that was inflicted upon you personally.

Sometimes the act that hurt us has nothing to do with the person in which committed it but rather, something deep inside of us. And when that action makes us feel something that we may have felt before and uncovers that root of insecurity, bitterness, jealousy, rejection, etc. that's already in us, we find ourselves wounded. For example, if a person doesn't invite you to an event that they have, or perhaps they walk past you and don't speak, and you get offended. Did they do something to you? Do they owe you an invite? Maybe their mind was on something when they walked past you and didn't speak. Are they the issue, or is your sensitivity the issue? Are you putting your rejection issues and feelings of invisibility off on someone who is not responsible for them? Really, ask yourself, what did they do to you? Did they genuinely do you a disservice, and even if they did, Jesus said the servant is not greater than his master? So if people dogged out Jesus, why do we feel as if we have the right to hold on to offense? I am not saying be okay with people treating you any kind of way, but what I am saying is don't allow people to cause you to embrace the title of victim. Get some spiritual backbone and maturity and learn how to properly handle these offenses that are sure to come. Everyone gets hurt. I am not saying you are immature if you get offended or if you get hurt. I am saying the way you handle it, how you internalize and process it speaks to your maturity or lack thereof.

HEAR ME PLEASE. I have had horrendous things happen to me by people who were supposed to have my best interest at heart. I am not discounting anyone's pain. I get it. Believe me. I have multiple stories of people intentionally trying to destroy me, trying to break me down, and their intentions were most definitely diabolical. Again, I understand that offense and pain is a very real and legitimate thing. But if we could ever get an understanding and grasp the whole picture, much of what we feel has broken us can empower us if we allow God to flip the script and let it work for our good. If we ever learned how to allow God to turn the pain into purpose.

At what point will we get tired of making our pain our god? At what point will we get tired of resting in victim-hood? At what point will we grow up in God? These are the things that I had to say to myself. When will we learn how to take a licking and keep on ticking? When will we silence the voice of the naysayers and stand up and be who God called us to be? We are soldiers in the army of the LORD. We said hurting people hurt people, so when will we be able to turn a situation around…and instead of swearing off the person that offended you, maybe we minister to them? Maybe it is the enemy that is trying to keep you at odds with someone because he knows you have the power to help them, or them you. If we could ever get to the point where we look at things from God's perspective…and instead of feeding into being mad at someone who we feel wronged us, what if we could turn around and minister to them in their brokenness because we can see pass what they did to us and why they did it? But if we are both broken and battered, nobody gets the victory but the devil. However, often, we are so self-involved we can't see (spiritually) pass what we see (naturally).

Next time you feel as if someone offends you, ask yourself what did they do to YOU to cause YOU to be offended? Is this offense something that was intentional on their part? Was it meant as an attack on you? If it is truly a legitimate offense, deal with it the way the Bible says to deal with it. Try to talk it out with them. If that doesn't work, take someone that is unbiased and wise with you. If that doesn't work, take a couple more people…and so on. But before doing all that, make sure that the issue IS NOT YOU FIRST. We must stop placing blame and be accountable. If we are going to make it in this thing called the church and the kingdom with our minds intact, we must learn to put things in proper perspective and stop seeing things through our skewed perception, fragile heart, and bed of emotions. We cannot control what people do and why, but what we absolutely must grab hold of is how we react. And not just how we react because we can have toxic thoughts in our mind and heart and not carry out any act, but the thoughts eat us up from the inside. We replay it over and over, trying to understand why, and the more time we are thinking on it, meditating on it, it is seeping into our spirits and strengthening the fortresses of bitterness, resentment, and brokenness that already exist. We must filter things through truth and God's Spirit. We must filter everything through God's Word. Utilize Philippians 4:8. We must grow up in God and quit taking everything so personal. Even if it was intentional…then that means the person who would purposely try to hurt you has an issue of the heart. Well, guess what? You do too. So pray for yourself and pray for that person while you're at it and keep it moving!

Do we not realize, a lot of these riffs and disagreements and fallouts are DISTRACTIONS from the enemy? It is meant to keep you off course. You are gaining too much ground, and he must stop you. He must put a monkey wrench in your progress. He senses the relationship might bless you, or it might bless the other person, so he tries to destroy it. Let's wake up and see what is really going on.

The thing we often miss is this: Romans 8:28 says, "All things work together for the good to them who love the LORD to them that are called according to his purpose." It did not say all the BIG things. It said, "All things work together for good to them that love God…" That means, if God allowed it…it is for a reason. Get your eyes off the person; don't direct your energy to the perceived wrong that they did to you. No, better use of your energy and focus is to ask YOURSELF why did it offend you? Why did it hurt your feelings? Most of the things that offend us shouldn't. Simple. But because we have issues, we put our issues on other people. Most of the times it is not even about them; it is about what you feel, is rejection. It is about your need for validation; it is about the insecurity that you have…THAT is the enemy. THAT is the thing that we need to be delivered from. God will allow certain things to happen, and we think it happened for one reason when the purpose was for something entirely different.

See, the Bible really does instruct us in all matters. But we pick and choose what we want to live by; we use what we want and dismiss other key principles. If we would do as the Bible says and cast all our burdens and cares upon Him because He cares for us, one of the things that would happen is you would tell God that this particular thing hurt your feelings. You would get it all out, be hurt, cry, tell Him how you were done wrong and etc., and then He could tell you why you are really hurt. He would be able to tell you why it really bothered you, and then right in His presence, in that exchange, you can give Him that bitterness, and He can give you truth and healing.

Remember, you will NEVER be able to control what people do or why…so it's best to start learning how to react to things. People will say things that will break you to your core.

People will try to abuse you, lie on you, mistreat you, and set you up. This is just the enemy using broken people. People that need help too, so pray for those that hurt you; deal with the spirit and love the people. Also, keep in mind that you too have once been the person to hurt someone. Remember that you cannot fight a spiritual battle in the flesh.

The enemy wants you to think that the enemy is your brother or sister, when in reality, it is him working behind the scenes...and if you will focus on trying to fight them, then you won't concentrate on trying to fight him, and please know: you can only fight the enemy in the spirit. For the weapons of our warfare are not carnal (so going off, giving people a piece of your mind, putting them in their place, etc....none of that will work because even if you do set them straight, the devil will just get somebody else to use against you, and you have fought your own battle, saying to God that you don't need Him because you got it...BUT YOU'RE FIGHTING the wrong thing, and you are fighting the wrong way). I am not your enemy, you are not my enemy, we are not each other's enemy; it is the devil, the world, and our own wretched flesh that is our enemy. That is why the Scripture goes on to say that the weapons of our warfare are mighty through God to the pulling down of strongholds.

We don't want to just be reactive, but we want to be pro-active. We want to do the necessary work up front that will allow us to avoid these negative situations. We can do this by regularly taking inventory of our own selves. See, if we spent as much time removing the beam out of our eye, we truly would not have enough time to point out the mote in our sister's or brother's eye.

Sometimes, God allows situations to happen because He is trying to remove something in us that should not be, and/or He is trying to work out strongholds in our mind or behaviors that shouldn't be and replace them with strongholds of truth. We spend time being hurt and unforgiving over a process that God is allowing to make us better and help us grow. Yes, it hurts. But it is indeed necessary.

Listen, if you are truly anointed…and I mean for real, if God has impregnated you with a real ministry that He wants to birth out of you, YOU CANNOT SKIP THE PROCESS. YOU MUST GO THROUGH EVERY STAGE of God's SPIRITUAL BOOT-CAMP to ensure that you can handle the mandate on your life. IT HURTS, it sucks, it's hard, it is lonely sometimes…but there is no way around the valley of death if you want to make it to the other side where God now manifests His power through you, and now you are able to speak life and cause dead and dry bones to come alive. Everything in you must be broken and built back up in Jesus to ensure the structural integrity and foundation on which the ministry in you will be built upon is solid.

From now on, try to see the issues you have with people as an opportunity for growth. Maybe there is an understanding or knowledge to be gained. Maybe it is to show forth the glory and power of Jesus. Be His branch. Let Him flow mercy, understanding, forgiveness, and love through you to the person that hurt or offended you. This is not to say they will always receive it, but believe me, if they are truly your brother and sister in Christ, you will leave a seed, and you would have left them with something to think about whenever they come to themselves. They may never acknowledge it, but you have done your part. At the point that you have self-evaluated, forgiven, done all you were led by God to do, and you extended the love of Christ, it is now between them and God. You should move on. Don't let people keep you bound with an offense. Give it to God and leave it with Him and ask Him to help you through it. If nothing else, pray for those that use and mistreat you. Every time conflict arises, use it as a chance to look inwardly first and assess yourself. If it is the enemy at work, remember…we war in the spirit and not the flesh. Your brother and your sister are not your enemies. This can be hard to understand sometimes when all you see when you look at their actions are Satan…but they are a soul. Take your anger out on the enemy. Don't fall into his trap by allowing your emotions to cause you to deal with things carnally. Before we react to an offense, pray.

We have been hurt, and we are likely to be hurt again. We have been disappointed, and we are likely to be disappointed again. People have broken our hearts, and there may be people who try to do it again. If we know that this will be the case, then we ought to start being proactive rather than reactive. We need to realize that internalizing and reacting to all the things the enemy is trying to throw at us will drive us mad if we let it. The enemy will constantly send offenses if he knows you will respond emotionally and allow it to control how you feel about yourself. If he knows that you will make decisions based on your emotions rather than the Spirit of God, he will try to constantly keep you at odds. He will try to send you in every direction but the right direction if he knows that we will be moved by what others do and say to us. We must put a stop to it. We can't control others, but we can control ourselves. So rather than being focused on what people say or do to us, we must see past that and focus on how we respond.

We must start guarding our heart before the offense comes because if you wait until afterward, you are a little late and might be subject to suffering more than you had to. Think of this: if you owned a bank that had millions of dollars in it, but you had no guards to protect it, someone is likely to break in, especially if they have observed that you have no security in place. You will not be able to prevent thieves from coming in if you have no guards securing the perimeter, so at the point that thieves break in, you are now on damage control. Any guards sent after the intrusion has already occurred is ultimately a cleanup crew.

Now, if armed guards patrolled the bank to begin with, you could have prevented the break-in and any damage that had been done as a result. Same with our hearts. Put safeguards in place now. Guard it now with the truth of God's Word, with His love, and being transformed by the renewing of your mind by thinking and meditating on His thoughts and on His Word and being focused on His will. It is true that if we keep our eyes on Jesus, a lot of what tries to come at us is inconsequential and rendered of no effect.

Being delivered from people really means you have gotten to a place where you are anchored in God's truth. You know who you are in God, and you know who He is in you. You allow His Spirit to rule and reign in you. You allow His thoughts and His truth to consume you. You are confident in your relationship with God and are confident of the fact that He resides in you and that He has a purpose for your life. When this happens, the opinions and actions of others will have little power over you.

CHAPTER 7

Watch Your Mouth

Life and death are in the power of the tongue. If we really understood the weight of this statement, we would be much more mindful of what we say. And not only what we say, but what we think and meditate on. The things we let into our spirit through our thoughts by constantly thinking of them get into our heart, and the Bible says out of the abundance of the heart the mouth speaks.

God, who is a Spirit, said, "Let there be light," and there was light. And He saw that it was good. God, who is a Spirit, spoke this world into existence, and that same God (if we have been filled with His Spirit) lives in us. God, who is Spirit…speaks, and what He speaks manifest. EVERY TIME. Every single time without fail. So if we, having God's Spirit in us (the same Spirit who spoke and the world was created) speak, we must understand that the words that come out of our mouth are infused with creative power. We have a hard time remembering or understanding this because the consequences or rewards of our words are not manifested immediately before our eyes. However, when we speak, there are unseen things happening.

Imagine for a moment that you had insight into the spirit realm. What if there were angels waiting and demons lurking, waiting for you to give them something to do? You speak, and your words that are infused with creative power are either snatched up by the angels or demons, depending on what it is you said. The enemy is not all-knowing, nor is he in every place at all times, but it does say he is the prince of the air...so, if you say something aloud, he is likely to hear you. **Would you still speak haphazardly and negatively about yourself if you knew that you were giving the enemy a "legal assignment" from you, to try and destroy you, or cause you some sort of emotional, mental, or physical discomfort or pain**? Would you purposely cooperate and furnish your enemy with weaponry against you?

Now just imagine what happens when you speak God's Word over your life. Think about what could happen if by faith, you spoke blessings and positivity over your life and the lives of others. Visualize the angels making haste to execute and carry out the assignment given, and ultimately it manifests in the natural.

We cannot be so careless with our words. There is an unseen realm that our words impact. If we speak negatively, we put our words out there to be heard by the enemy and his camp. Do you realize that he will work ferociously to carry out whatever would kill, steal from you, or destroy you, especially if you gave him permission because YOU SAID IT? We give him a legal right when we speak negativity to carry it out. And unless your negative words are intercepted through prayer and rendered powerless, you now are responsible for the destruction that your words will eventually cause you.

Positive words that are in line with God's will for you, words of faith, and God's Word will propel you forward. The negativity we speak will always pull us back; and therefore, sometimes, we find ourselves stuck or stagnant. We speak by faith the Word of God, so we start to make progress, then when something doesn't happen like we think it should, or something comes out of left field and looks contrary to what you are believing for, instead of us digging in, pressing into faith even the more, we speak out of our flesh, our negative emotions, negative thoughts, and some of that ground we gained we now lose, thus, finding ourselves stuck and unable to advance because we are double-minded. This right here is the devil's playground.

Faith is not feeling. If the enemy knows you will cancel out the blessing God has for you with your mouth because of what you feel, he will play you like a puppet on a string for as long as you will allow, and he will consistently set a snare for you in this area to cause you to speak negatively out of what you feel instead of positively out of faith.

We must learn how to control our mouths no matter how we feel. In spite, and sometimes because of what we feel, we must learn how to use our mouth to build up, encourage, praise, worship, declare, and war (spiritually). We must be intentional, strategic, and mindful of what we say, especially when we are in our feelings. We are at war; it would behoove us to start thinking like soldiers. Know your enemy, know the tactics he uses, be mindful of how he tries to pull your strings to get you to forfeit your blessings and act out of character. But more importantly, know your God and what His Word says about you, and develop a relationship with Him so you can get a rhema (fresh, right now, tailor-made) word for your situation and speak that.

Your life will follow your words. BE CAREFUL. What direction are you trying to go in?

If you are always speaking defeat, complaining, doubting, and fearing, your life will surely follow and manifest what you speak. If you speak victory, appreciation, trust, faith, your life will surely follow and manifest what you speak. YOU DECIDE.

Sometimes an even bigger problem is not what we say about ourselves but what we say about others. Be honest. I mean, really think about your conversations. Yes, maybe you don't talk about people in front of mixed company, but what is your conversation sounding like when you are around your inner circle? To thine own self be true. We are not fooling anyone but ourselves. We might as well be honest, tell the truth, and shame the devil. If we can't grow, if we can't work on the beam in our own eye, if we cannot admit and own up to our faults, we make the Holy Ghost of no effect in our lives. Not because it is powerless, but because we refuse to tap into the power it affords us to continually be transformed into the image of Jesus by crucifying this wretched flesh. It takes strength to admit our faults AND then do something about them.

Nobody is perfect. We all have issues that we are working on, and sometimes understanding the detrimental and devastating effects of our actions will aid us in making better decisions.

Have you ever stopped and asked yourself, "Why am I talking about this person?" "Is it because I am jealous?" "Is it because they offended me?" "Is it because they intimidate me?" "Is it because I do not understand them?" "Is it because it makes me feel better about myself to put them down?" "Is it because I have deep-seated insecurities that I didn't even realize I had, so I developed this skill of faultfinding?" How does this glorify God?

Speaking down about somebody, gossiping, spreading lies about people, and speaking any kind of negativity about anybody that God loves serves you no purpose whatsoever. As a matter of fact, it is detrimental to **your** spiritual health… yet we do it anyway. Whether you are the speaker or the listener, if you are in the company of someone who is speaking directly to you, and they are talking negatively about someone else and you don't say anything or you let it continue without stopping it in some way, you are an accomplice and are complicit in this evil communication. We should just repent right now because at one time or another, we all have been guilty of this. But at some point, we must grow up; at some point, we must understand the consequences of our actions.

There used to be this saying "Sticks and stones may break my bones, but words will never hurt me." That is a lie from the pit, if I ever heard one. Again, life and death are in the power of the tongue; our words can wound a person to their core. Words have started wars; words have caused people to lose their lives; words have caused people to kill themselves; words have caused people to live their whole lives feeling unworthy; words have caused people to live their whole life in defeat.

But also, words have ended wars and brought peace; words have given life; words have healed; words have delivered; words have encouraged; words have empowered; words have caused people to believe they can do the impossible; words have caused people to accomplish goals they thought were unattainable. Words can be used for good, and they can be used for bad. If you are a child of God, our choice should always be to use our words for good. Be a builder instead of a destroyer. Choose to build people up in God in lieu of tearing them down.

Another area that we need to really be careful of is when we put our mouth on our leaders. I could write a whole book on this, and one day maybe I will. But for now, I will say this: JUST DO NOT DO IT. We need to watch our words and our conversation when we are speaking on matters that we don't have all the information on. If God hasn't spoken to you or given you godly discernment (and it is not discernment when your heart is not right) or godly insight, or if you have not heard things from the horse's mouth, it would serve us best to be silent.

Sometimes, we just talk too much. We have an opinion about everything, and we do not know what we are talking about. There is a saying that I always liked, and that is "It is better to be thought a fool than to open up your mouth and confirm that you are." Even if a leader is a low-down dirty dog, what does it serve you to dog them out? Again, motive is everything. If you are warning people about this leader because souls are in jeopardy and because the leader is dangerous to the body of Christ (and you are being led of the LORD), that is one thing…but there is a difference in telling facts and running somebody down. The truth is the truth, but even then, be mindful of why you are doing what you are doing, and make sure God approves.

Now if He does, that is another matter. For the sake of this point, I am talking about real men and women of God.

Listen, we are all human. Nobody but Jesus is perfect. Even leaders have faults, flaws, and even they make mistakes sometimes. But afford them the same mercy you want God to give you. With that being said, men and women of God are not just your ordinary run-of-the-mill people. We must be careful and handle them with care. If you don't agree with your leaders, pray. If you have an issue with them, pray and seek God before you act and before you speak. If you want to talk about them, gossip about them, or run them down to your friends and family, DON'T. You are hurting yourself more than you are hurting that leader.

And another thing, if you genuinely love your friends and your family, why would you include them in on your destruction? **If you are determined to speak negatively about the leaders that God placed you under and that you chose, then fine, but something is wrong with your love if you bring other people in the mix and make them an accomplice.**

Friends protect their friends. There have been several times, a situation existed, where I was angry and broken because of what I felt a leader did to me. But if you asked my very best friends, they couldn't even tell you anything that happened. It's because they would be none the wiser; they would not know what you are talking about, and it's not because I have so much integrity or am so good, but it is because I understood that it was dangerous, plus I understand that blood would be on my hands if they borrow my offense and now become angry or started seeing a leader through the picture that I paint for them.

Now, what if later on down the line, when I have forgiven the leader or they have forgiven me, my friend or family member who knew I went through something with this leader is now going through something with this same leader, and by example, I showed them it is okay to put their mouth on them. Now, what if the information they compiled from me, along with other experiences, cause them to leave a ministry or church…and what if that is the wrong decision for that person? Now, you can't control people, but I wouldn't want anything at all that I have said or done to contribute to someone making a faulty decision. No, MA'AM, NO, SIR, you will not use my experiences to validate and justify your bad and ungodly decisions. Also, what if "I" was wrong? Now someone else has considered the erroneous information that was given to them by a person who was operating out of emotion rather than truth and the wisdom of God.

Be careful of what you share and why. Everyone needs someone to talk to, but do you really need to discuss it with five or ten different people? Be wise about the person or people you choose to share information with. Make sure they are unbiased, wise, and love God and His righteousness more than they love you. Make sure they are loyal to God more than they are loyal to you or anyone else. The best thing to do would be to ask God who you should talk to.

The next time you are engaged in a conversation that you think might be questionable, just ask yourself what is the purpose of the conversation, why are you having it, and what do you hope to accomplish out of it. When it is all said and done, your words will bless or curse you. If you want to be blessed, speak well of yourselves and others.

I also want to stress watching our mouth as it relates to communication in other forms. Whether that be communicating through facial expressions, or conveying your messages through e-mail or text. Still be mindful of what you are conveying to another, and how you are conveying it. I remember something the Lord told me years ago. I was at work sitting at my desk when I received an e-mail that angered me so much my head started sweating. I was raging within and had to respond. I was typing so intensely I couldn't get the words out fast enough; I needed to make sure that the e-mail was politically correct on the surface with all kinds of shots fired in the undertone. I was angry, and I needed to release that on my intended target but in a way where I covered myself. So I read it again to make sure it was saying everything I wanted it to say and that you could feel my anger without me having to state it.

Just before I could press send, God impressed on my spirit and said, "**Don't let anything come out of your mouth that My Spirit did not get a chance to edit**." And just like that, I realized I was not going to get the satisfaction of my intended target reading this e-mail that I had just put all this effort into carefully crafting. I was sick, not literally, but I felt like it… I battled…because I really wanted to send that e-mail…BUT God! Sometimes we don't realize the full consequences or fallout of our actions.

See, later at that same job, the LORD used me to get about twenty of the women that worked there to come to our church prayer breakfast—women of all nationalities and positions within the organization. Most were either supervisors or managers. I remember one of those same ladies who was a manager called me into her office. She was going up for a promotion and wanted me to pray for her. See, after that prayer breakfast, several of the ladies would come to me from time to time and seek counsel or prayer, and therein was my opportunity to share Jesus with them and to minister to their souls. That door would not have been opened had I sent that e-mail because I probably would have been fired. Even if I did not get fired the word would have gotten around, and I am sure I would have been looked at a different way.

The devil uses traps to get you to lose your witness. But because I listened to God, killed my flesh, and submitted to what He said, I did not allow those words to be sent, which in turn allowed God's light to shine.

See, sometimes our mouth or actions can cause us to lose things we never knew we would have received or cause us to lose out on Him using us in a way that we never imagined. We don't know what we lost because we never got it; our mouth canceled it before we could get it. I wonder all the things that never came to us or all the things that never happened in the past because of our mouths.

So I plead with you, watch your words. Be careful what you say, and be careful with the conversations you have and who you have them with.

Speak what Jesus says about you, what He says about others, and what He says about your situation. Jesus says that you are the apple of His eye. He says that you are above and not beneath—the head and not the tail. He says you are fearfully and wonderfully made. Jesus says that eyes have not seen nor ears have heard neither has it entered into the heart of men the things that He has in store for you. Jesus says be confident that He who began a good work in you will perfect it and complete it. He says that His strength is made perfect in your weakness. He says that many are the afflictions of the righteous but He is able to deliver you out of them all. He says that your light affliction, which is but for a moment is working (producing) a far more exceeding eternal weight of glory. He says that we are troubled on every side yet not distressed, perplexed but not in despair, persecuted but not forsaken, cast down but not destroyed. **God says blessings and cursing coming out of the same mouth** SHOULD NOT BE!

CHAPTER 8

"Church Hurt"

I remember I was about to enter what probably was one of the hardest and most painful trials and test of my life since being saved. The devil tried to get me to take my life because of this situation…BUT GOD!

Long story short, there was a leader that I looked up to that totally turned on me just like Saul did with David. They tried to kill me spiritually and assassinate my character. People were intimidated by them, so for fear of having issues with them, they submitted to what they were told. This person sat me down from working with them in a ministry, and people in the church were not allowed to speak to me or deal with me, and if you did, they would have a conversation with you as to encourage you not to. Why, you ask? Simply put, it was the enemy.

Before things went "left," however, this leader was my mentor. I was their assistant director of a ministry that they were over. They were the very person who constantly urged me to go tell my pastor about the prophetic call on my life. Matter of fact it was when they discovered that about me that they took to me. I looked up to them. I only wanted to learn from them, and even though I knew what they were doing to me was not right, I still loved them; I still protected them. I was told that this person antagonized me so because they were jealous. I didn't understand it at the time because I thought they were the greatest thing since sliced bread. I loved them, and I admired the way God used them. I was drawn to their depth of knowledge on spiritual warfare and how God used them prophetically. So all I wanted to do was learn from them, sit at their feet, and they were determined to break me.

I remember a minister, who is now a pastor, asked me to be one of the altar workers when our organization would have our youth services. I asked my assistant pastor, who asked my pastor, and I got the okay. This person that was determined to persecute me, saw my name on a program as an altar worker, and went to the minister who originally asked me to work in that capacity and told him I did not have permission and made it look as if I was being sneaky and being a rebel. I could not tell him that this person was being driven by a wicked spirit and that they were not telling the truth. Every time I saw the minister, I had to look at that man and let him think I was guilty of whatever this person had told him, and I could not go to him and make it right. The Lord had told me in prayer that He would justify, so while going through this whole ordeal, I never took up for myself or discussed it with anyone not involved. My assistant pastor, who was aware that this happened, called me and just apologized. He tried to get this person to come to their senses, but they were relentless in trying to destroy me.

BUT GUESS what? Knowing all he knew, my assistant pastor told me that I was still responsible for being this person's spiritual armor-bearer. Even though this person was determined to kill me, he instructed me to pray for them. He made me go to the services that they preached at to cover them in prayer. I would go and they would be preaching about me over the pulpit while I was right there, and everyone knew it. Yet he still made me go. I COULD NOT BELIEVE THIS. You mean to tell me that I had to pray for this person who was dogging me out, lying on me, doing everything to kill my spirit in hopes that I would kill myself? For the life of me, I didn't understand why I had to subject myself to this treatment. My thinking was I could pray for them from home. Why do I have to go to a service where I know that they are going to be calling me the devil over the pulpit? I could not understand…but in hindsight, I am forever grateful for the counsel that my assistant pastor (my mentor) at the time gave me. It taught me to fight through persecution and to not run. It taught me to walk out difficult situations; it gave me a spiritual fortitude that I could not have gained in seminary alone. If I could stay in the fire for years without running, I could endure anything with the help of the Lord.

My mentor was teaching me strength and honor. He was teaching me warfare. I can go toe to toe with the enemy IN THE NAME OF JESUS without being fearful because of what I went through. I have taken down giants through the spirit of GOD…but to do that, you must do it GOD's way, and that is what I was learning. He would tell me to never let this person see me cry, not to put my head down, but to dust myself off and show up no matter what. God was using my mentor to make a soldier out of me.

I was blessed. A lot of people go through things in the church and can't see how positivity can come from it, and they don't have anyone helping to navigate them through.

They don't even understand why it was allowed, and because of this they are lost, confused, and blaming the wrong entity.

The church did not hurt you. Yes, we the people are considered the church, but the entity itself did not hurt you. The church that Jesus established, the purpose and intent of the organization or kingdom that we know as the church, is not what hurt you; it is members or people that attend the established entity that hurt you. We experience bullying, rejection, trauma, our first heartbreak at school, but do we forsake it? Did the school hurt us, or was it someone who attended the school that hurt us? Do you cease to learn because you were hurt at a school? In the workplace, bosses harass, embarrass, coworkers plot and set snares, do we forsake our job and say we will never work again because we were hurt at work?

In our family, we are hurt, used, abused, and neglected, but do we forsake our family? Even if you do in action, they don't cease to be your family by law. So why, when we get hurt by people who attend church, some of us try to write church off altogether, or we leave the church we attend? Sometimes that is necessary, but I believe that time is few and far in between. We need to learn to ride things out, to let the process take its course so that we may learn and be made.

Now, I am not oblivious to the fact that if a child goes to school and is hurt by a teacher, then the school is often held liable. If a worker goes to their place of employment and is violated by someone in management or leadership, the company could be held liable. So I understand that the same applies as it relates to us being hurt by people who attend or are to represent the church. The person who hurt you is a member just like you are, and while they may have authority, they were not representing the church if what they did was a sin. They were representing their flesh, and that is where the blame lies, not on the church. All I am saying is don't allow the enemy to run you away from the place that is meant to help you. That is a trick of the enemy. If the offense is so egregious that staying would cause you to die spiritually, then ask God to lead you to where you need to be, and don't leave until He gives instruction. Sometimes we think we are dying when we aren't. God knows what we can handle.

I also must make this point, and it is a hard pill to swallow but it is the truth, nevertheless. If I, being an adult, engage in behavior that is displeasing to God, and I get caught or either the fallout of my actions cause situations to occur in which offend or hurt me, at what point do I take responsibility for the fact that if I had never done what I knew to be wrong in the first place, then I would not have experienced the aftermath and fallout from my actions? It is true. Often people who engage in the same act are disproportionately disciplined. This can be for various reasons, and most may be unfair. However, let's say, my friend and I rob a bank and we both beat up a guard. We get caught and our lawyers want to try our cases separately. I get fifteen years, and my friend who had a different lawyer, different jury and judge gets five years. Is that unfair? Maybe, but I would not be in jail at all if I did not rob the bank. This point can be argued until kingdom come, but the fact remains that sometimes things are just unfair, and if we spend our life being bitter and sour over the things we deem to be unfair instead of first taking responsibility if there is any to take, and then finding a way to move on, then we will be imprisoned and allowing the situation to hold even more power over us.

We need to be careful not to mistake the actions and heart of men to be the intent and heart of God. Those two things are separate. Those in authority, and those that represent the church, should be fair, honest, holy, above board in every way. Is this the case all the time? No! In those times, we have the Holy Spirit that can help navigate us through the situation. Let the Spirit of God lead you, not your flesh. That is what I am trying to get across.

Sometimes it looks as if people are getting away with something, and they aren't. It could be God allowing grace for them to get it together, just like He allowed with you. We can't gauge how, when, and to what degree people should be punished for wronging you, just like people we wronged didn't get the last say on how we were to be dealt with. Even if you think they did, nothing more than what God allowed could have happened to you, and the same with the person that caused you hurt.

God's business is His business. You do not touch His anointed; you do not get to decide who is His anointed and who is not His anointed. Saul was wicked and constantly tried to kill David, yet David considered him God's anointed. Even in my situation, I started to question my worth because I could not understand why God would allow me to be hurt and persecuted like this, and I did nothing at all to this person. I asked them years later when we had a talk, and they still could not tell me what I did. They did not know. But I understood it was the enemy, and I forgave the person although I am still dealing with the some of the fragments of that ordeal even now. However, I felt like…it still didn't matter. I was not to touch God's anointed even though I was God's anointed too. Matter of fact, even more so. See, I came to understand that how I went through that ordeal is what would either set me up for promotion from the Lord years later or what would have testified against it had I tried to fight in my own power.

My hurt was no excuse or justification to put my mouth on them even though THEY WERE WRONG.

I put this story in here for people who say they have church hurt. Before I went into this subject, I needed you to understand I am familiar with hurt inflicted for the most diabolical of reasons. I want you to know that I am not talking out of the side of my mouth. If anybody knows about what people call church hurt, it would be me. Try having a person turn your whole church against you, with nobody on your side but your pastor and assistant pastor. Imagine having to deal with the closest people to you turning their back on you while you are going through this persecution. What about someone you considered family believing what this person who was trying to destroy you was telling them? And the only thing that could change your own family member's mind, the one that God used to bring you into the church, was that GOD Himself had to let them know it wasn't what they were thinking. It took God to speak up for me; otherwise, everyone would have turned their backs. Till this day, I don't think everyone involved fully understood what happened, but it was the enemy. I had people throwing me under the bus for fear that this leader would think they were on my side. It was not until years later when God sent me somewhere else, and then these same people who thought it was me (remember, I did not speak up for myself) experienced some of the same things at the hand of this leader that I did. It wasn't until then that some of them had an "ah-hah" moment. I had to forgive them, and some of the people that turned on me never asked me for forgiveness, but I forgave them anyway, and we developed a relationship again.

See, I didn't blame them although it hurt me in ways they could never understand. No one had the courage to stand up for what was right for fear of this person. My pastor would try to shield me, my assistant pastor would try and fight for me, but this was a spirit of Jezebel, and I'm not sure many knew what they were really dealing with. But I did, and that is why the enemy had to shut me up. That is why the attack was so ferocious against me. See, this leader knew about the prophetic call on my life. I had prophesied to them; I had prophesied to their sister; I had recalled a whole conversation that they had with GOD word for word. I was so green at the time I didn't even know what I was doing was prophesying. I was just telling them what I saw and what I heard in prayer. They identified a prophetic call on my life and latched on to me until the gift that they recognized could expose them. I don't even think they knew why they were turning on me. It was the enemy who feared being exposed. When they were in their right mind, we were okay. It was so bad people were not allowed to speak to me. The children of the family really could not make out what was going on; they only knew what they were told, and of course, they believed their family, so even the kids were threatening me, and again, I didn't blame them. They didn't know any better and, to this day, probably still don't realize that their family member was wrong. I remember one time, I was being attacked, and I was having pain in my body. I went up to the altar at a service where this person was ministering, and mostly everybody on the altar was a part of their crew, so I went up to get prayer and in front of the whole church. One by one the altar workers would step back and would not pray for me. This happened in front of a whole church; thankfully someone else finally prayed for me.

I know about being hurt by people who attend church, especially those that are supposed to be leaders. This leader who made it their duty to assassinate me even told me that they saw me killing myself. They laid it out, play by play. We weren't in a good place. They were persecuting me, so why would they tell me that they saw me committing suicide? They were being used by the enemy to try and put thoughts in my mind and to put a curse on me, and they didn't even realize it. Or maybe they did. I don't know. But it seemed as if this person was okay with seeing me dead just so they can say they were right or to get me out of their way. This person wanted to run the church and anything that got in their way or that they thought would challenge that had to go...and that meant me. See, before any of this happened, God had given me several dreams—about the spirit of Jezebel, about the attacks that were about to happen on the pastor and this person who was attacking me. Even after everything that was done to me, for whatever reason, at that time, even though I knew what they were doing was evil, I still placed stock in this person. I still believed that they were God's anointed and that in some way they were greater than me or meant more to God than I did. So if it had not been for God, their words could have sent me to my death.

But still, I must say, **the church did not hurt me**. This person who was broken hurt me. I don't blame them either; they were attacked and succumbed to it. They allowed themselves to be used by the enemy. I really believe this leader had an open door of resentment, unforgiveness, jealousy, bitterness, or something that allowed this spirit to infiltrate and take over.

However, truth be told, we too may have been used by the enemy at one point or another to hurt someone. Now, maybe not to this degree, but nonetheless, none of us are perfect. This person who was persecuting me needed prayer.

They needed someone warring on their behalf even though they were trying their best to kill me. When I think back, this person was really going through some challenging times in their life. A family member was battling with an illness. Their desires of greatness and to travel the world and be known had not come to fruition. They were going through changes personally, and somehow, there was a door of discontentment and/or resentment that creeped in. I believe, since they couldn't get the glory and recognition by doing what they always wanted to do, the sacrifice they made instead caused them to become disgruntled, and when this spirit entered in its lust for power and position took over. Again, this person needed prayer. At the heart of what was going on was the fact they had not dealt with some disappointment and maybe some hurt. Remember, hurting people hurt other people.

Listen, in the kingdom of GOD, we need to start exercising some real power. Not this powder puff image of sainthood. The apostles died for the Gospel; the apostles died trying to save souls of the very people that were persecuting them. Jesus forgave the people that tried to kill Him. He died for those that betrayed Him and called for His life. But Jesus understood that there was something greater at work here. Jesus said that no one had the power to take His life. No, He laid it down willingly. For the joy that was set before Him, He endured the cross and despised the shame. Same with you, nobody has the power to take your life. Nobody should be able to break you so that you cannot recover. Jesus paid too much for that not to be so.

We must be able to take some things. Okay, people hurt our feelings, but what are we going to do about it? Retaliate? Remain wounded? Or feel the hurt and deal with it appropriately by giving it to God, and in exchange, He can give you forgiveness, strength, resilience, and peace? If we can't take people lying on us, rejecting us, betraying us, talking about us, then we can't take life. But guess what? All that happened to Jesus and He did not run. Jesus says the servant is not greater than his master, so why don't we get this? His Word says that we are accounted for as sheep for the slaughter all day long. This walk is not for the faint at heart. If you want to be saved for real, if you want to experience the power of God for real, if you ever want to be used by God in a mighty way, guess what? This is your portion. You can't escape the process. These things happen whether you are saved or not. Thank God that with Him, we have the ability to overcome and handle situations with wisdom and in turn, gain strength and insight.

People want to leave the church because someone they dated is now dating someone else. What? Really? People scream church hurt because you got sat down or got looked over for promotion. No one has experienced more "church hurt" than Jesus. He died for the church. Yet the very people that He died for so that they could become a part of the church wanted to kill Him, and still He ministered and offered salvation to those that persecuted Him. Jesus was our example; what He did we are to do.

So what if we really lived Scripture out in our life? What if we try to see past the hurt that someone causes us and try to understand why, and then minister to them where they are? Will this work all the time? No. But should you be willing? Yes. What if you prayed for the people that lied on you? What if you became an example for the people that disappointed you and that you thought should be an example for you? What if you stick it out, trust God, and let Him show His hand in your situation?

If you run, God does not get the glory. Now are there times when a situation calls for you to leave a church, yes, but even in that, if at all possible...don't leave broken. Don't leave bitter. Don't leave the wrong way, and only leave because GOD says so, not because you think your time is up, and not because you can't handle it. Rather, ask GOD to help you. Truth is, there may be days, weeks, months, even years where you will struggle, but don't let that deter you. Keep pressing, keep fighting, keep advancing, and walk it out. I'm telling you, those of you that can endure this test will have a reward and blessing waiting on the other side of it that will blow your mind. Let me ask you this: If you knew that at the end of your test (however long that may be), God would prepare a table for you in the presence of your enemies (your enemies being Satan and all those who serve him, not your brothers and sisters in Christ), would you endure? If you would give your pain and disappointments to GOD, if you would allow Him to heal you and walk you through the tough times and carry you in the valleys, would you endure if you knew GOD would bless you? Well, I am telling you now He will bless you. If the blessing is just that it draws you closer to GOD, then isn't it worth it? If the blessing is a manifestation of an anointing that could have only come through you enduring the process, wouldn't it be worth it? Do not make a permanent and destiny-altering decision out of a temporary emotion.

There is so much I would have missed if I left in the middle of my trial. So much I would not have learned, and most likely, I would have had to go through another situation that would have taught me similar lessons. I am not saying GOD caused anyone to try and hurt me, but I am saying that GOD allowed it, and if He allowed it, it was for a reason. And really, that should be good enough, but it never is for us. In that whole situation, I obtained wisdom, insight, and knowledge that I could not have gotten from reading in a book. I got war wounds that I am proud of because I have seen firsthand how that situation has caused me to help other people, and it is in times like that where GOD can use something that was miserable to us, something that was so painful to help someone else.

The Lord has allowed me to minister to leaders when they were also going through diabolical situations—situations that they didn't feel comfortable talking to people about. See, I understood exactly where they were. I would not have had the insight or experience to be able to help them had I not fought and encountered this spirit. The person in which the enemy uses is not your enemy; it's SATAN that is your adversary. When we can come to terms with this, it will keep us from fruitless battles. I do not go into battle unless I will win. I do not go into battle unless I am going to accomplish what I set out to accomplish, and finally, but foremost…after many lessons learned, I do not go into battle without GOD. This is what we need to learn. Sometimes what we call church hurt is no more than "the process." How can I say I have a deliverance ministry, a ministry in which I am on the front lines and war with formidable foes if I have never walked through or faced any giants? How can you walk someone else through it, if you don't know what you are talking about?

Now when you compare what some of us call church hurt against having someone try to kill your spirit and the enemy using them to try and cause you to commit suicide, well, you be the judge. Some things are just child's play. This is in no way to negate people's pain. Even if you were hurt because someone didn't speak to you, your hurt is real. I am not saying it isn't. What I am saying is you must get past that, deal with it properly, and not allow it to keep you bound. You must gain control over your emotions and not let your emotions control you. A lot of what we suffer is the enemy causing distractions. If he can keep you hurt, if he can keep you wounded, if he can keep you offended, if he can keep you bound in your mind and weak in your spirit, you will never rise up and operate in your full potential.

I believe that I had a reason to leave that church after years of persecution, but I did not have a word from the Lord. So I had to remain years after this person decided to destroy me. However, if I had left before the Lord sent me, I may have ended up at the wrong place. I did not join another church until I saw my current pastor on television. I did not know anything about him. I had never been to his church, plus it was on the opposite side of town, and I did not have a car at the time. I would watch him along with two other pastors on television, and one day, while watching him, God said, "Go there." And He told me that He was sending me there to be healed and trained. I met my husband at that church—the husband who loved me to life, who spoke life to dead and dry bones, the husband who would prophesy over me and who would ultimately encourage me and walk me through writing this book. The sovereignty of God is everything…and if you give it rule in your life, the rewards far outweigh the bad. Timing and location are everything when you are waiting on the manifestation of a blessing and when you are pursuing God's will for your life. Somehow all the pieces seem to fit together when you leave it to the master.

Some of the other things that we call church hurt is no more than the fruits of a wrong or disobedient decision that we made. At some point, we must stop blaming others and take accountability. I have been hurt, you have been hurt, we all have been hurt, but do we want to stay in that place, or do we want victory over the things that hurt us? It is a choice to either be a victim or a victor.

At the end of the day, we can't use church hurt as excuse to not attend church. That is not GOD. We cannot use church hurt as a reason to stay in our shell and not allow God to use us, on judgment day that excuse will not fly because GOD has given us everything we need to overcome. Church hopping for better opportunities is not GOD; that is you. So just be real and call things what they are, and let's quit putting our decisions off on GOD as if we were instructed by Him and using church hurt as a justification to go and do what our flesh is itching to do.

Finally, to those who have been genuinely hurt by leaders or your brothers and sisters in Christ, I am so sorry. I know what that feels like. While I have no authority to apologize for the people that proclaim to represent the church at large, I am sorry that you were wounded. Seek GOD, seek wise counsel, and don't make a move until you are clear that it is GOD talking and not your emotions. I am praying for you—praying that you will allow GOD to heal you and get the glory out of your situation. I am praying that you hide yourself in Jesus. I will tell you this, if you let GOD use you for His glory, it will hurt, but it will be worth it. He can flip the script and use your misery to propel you into your ministry. His strength can be made perfect in your weakness. Forgive the ones who hurt you. Forgive yourself if need be. Cry, give it to GOD, then wipe your tears, get up, and go conquer. Let the devil know that you see him. He tried it, but you didn't let him win.

CHAPTER 9

Forgiveness

I could not write a book about things that we may encounter, things that may take us off course, or things that we may come up against and not know how to handle, without speaking on forgiveness. The ability to truly forgive is an integral part of a successful walk with the LORD. However, it is one of the things we battle with the most. Heartbreakingly, I believe this will be the spiritual death of a lot of people, and if not rectified, it can be the thing that keeps you eternally separated from Jesus and out of heaven. It is in the Word of God that if we do not forgive others, then our Father that is in heaven will not forgive us. He also tells us that we are to forgive seventy times seven. These are not just words on a page. It is not a suggestion or advice. It is a command. And if we love Jesus, then we are to obey. We can't say that we love God but refuse to obey Him. He says that if you love Him, you will obey His commandments. If Jesus asks us to forgive, ideally, we will just do it because He instructs us to. But this is not always the case. There are times when we face things that seem unforgivable and the ability or the know-how of forgiveness escapes us, but try anyway.

For those that find yourself in a situation now where you need to forgive, and you are hurting, broken, confused, angry, or all the above…and the love of God that reigns in your heart is causing you to try and forgive, may God strengthen you, bless you, and enable you to completely forgive. Keep praying, keep asking God to give you a clean heart and a pure spirit. Ask God to help you stay in His presence so that He can operate on your heart, spirit, and mind and remove the offense and administer healing to your soul. I'm praying that God gives you the ability to genuinely forgive. It will help when you realize that you too have offended. And while you may feel that you have not done to another what has been done to you, you have hurt others nonetheless, and you understand this. You may also understand that you may have been hurting, broken, angry, or you may have not understood what you were doing at the time that you hurt someone; maybe this is the case of the person that hurt you. Hopefully, you have repented of the offense and hurt you caused others in your past. If you did, then God forgave you, and it is with this mindset ever before you that will help you to forgive those that have caused you pain. So I pray that God will give insight that will help you release the blame and the need for punishment to be rendered. Forgiveness is often a process, and I am praying that you will allow God to walk you through it to its completion so that He may get the glory.

To those who don't want to forgive, feel like you don't know how to forgive even if you wanted to, or to those who absolutely refuse to forgive, please know and understand that unforgiveness is hurting you more than the person it is directed toward. There is a saying: "**Unforgiveness is like taking poison and expecting someone else to die.**" There is so much truth in this. Unforgiveness can literally cause you to become ill, depressed, and bound. Unforgiveness also steals joy, possibilities, time, and quality of life. Unforgiveness prevents the power of God from operating in your life as it could. Unforgiveness skews your perspective and often causes us to make wrong decisions, and sometimes those decisions are life-altering and not for the better. Unforgiveness kills, destroys, tarnishes, and breaks. It causes darkness to hover over you, and it taints your heart. Pride makes us believe that unforgiveness is a justifiable act. But that is because you rejected the truth, and now your refusal to forgive has opened the door for delusion to enter, and you now begin to genuinely believe the lie you tell yourself. **The refusal to forgive is rebellion**. The Bible likens disobedience to witchcraft. We are disobeying a direct command from God. When we believe that we know better than God, or we are deceived into believing that God does not understand our hurt and agony, we are in trouble.

If you want to be forgiven, if you want to be able to commune with the Lord, if you want to live in His presence, if you want to be in right standing with God, forgiveness is a requirement. Often, the heartbreak we experience as a result of a traumatic situation outweighs our desire to obey God. But what you don't want is to make the pain, hurt, or anger you have suffered an idol and regard it more than you do the will of God. His will is for you to forgive. Most of us don't forgive because we want to; we forgive because we must. We understand that by not forgiving, we are in jeopardy of bringing judgment on ourselves. We know that we cannot expect God to forgive us, much less bless us, if we are harboring offense and unforgiveness in our hearts. The thing we fail to remember is that God loves us more than we love ourselves. He knows that unforgiveness is detrimental to us. He knows the destruction that it can cause, and it also prevents Him from moving in us the way He needs to. However, it is so much more powerful when you are in a place that your heart wants to forgive…no matter what. The type of people who love mercy, forgive swiftly (no matter the offense), are the type of people that God can trust and use even more mightily.

It glorifies God and speaks to His power working in your life when you can be broken, betrayed, misused, abused, persecuted, rejected, abandoned, lied to, or afflicted, and you choose to forgive the person who brought the offense. And when you not only forgive but choose to pray for them, and not only pray for them but you choose to love and allow God to be exemplified through you by looking for an open door to show that person Jesus and minister to them. Do you realize what kind of life-giving power that you are allowing God to show through you? The act of simply forgiving and not regarding your feelings but looking at the need of the person who hurt you and asking God if there is an open door to minister to help the one that hurt you—how powerful would that be? I wonder what kind of strongholds and yokes could be destroyed if we would choose to reject the enemy's temptation to keep us bitter and broken, if we would reject the temptation to wallow in the pain and look for purpose. What if Jesus was truly our Lord? What if we really meant it when we told God that He could use us in whatever way He wanted to and that we would do whatever He ask us to do because we understood that the life that we are living was bought and paid for by His blood? The life-giving, soul-redeeming blood of Jesus.

How dare we not forgive? Is the servant greater than his master? The answer to that question is NO! Jesus is not asking us to do something that isn't good for us. If we really think about it, it does nothing but help us when we forgive; it is beneficial to us in every way. We lose nothing except for the things we need to lose when we forgive. We lose bitterness, we lose pride and our right to administer or call for judgment, we lose wrong thinking, we lose the anger, and we end the separation between us and God. We only win when we forgive. You are not betraying anyone if you forgive. Lord forbid, someone took the life of your loved one; as hard as it is, you still must forgive. If you were in a relationship where you gave your all, you altered your life to help build up someone else, and you helped their dreams come true, but then they left you or betrayed you—as hard as it is, you must forgive. You must forgive that spouse or ex-spouse that hurt you. You must forgive that boss that did you dirty. You must forgive those friends that betrayed you and/or turned their backs on you. You must forgive that mother or father that wasn't what you needed them to be. I know it made your life much harder…but you made it. Let them go. I know that leader hurt you, misused you, and manipulated you; you must forgive. I know they stole your innocence, and that was something you could never get back, I understand. It happened to me too, several times…but you must forgive.

I know you may have had some diabolical things happen to you, and you lost years trying to understand the "why," but today is the day for you to forgive and let it go. Some things we will never understand. **Often, you will have to forgive when the person or people that have hurt you haven't even apologized or show no remorse**. Listen, don't wait for them to apologize before you forgive. You are stealing valuable time from yourself. No, forgive now, for your sanity and for your benefit. We let unforgiveness steal so much from us…so much that we could have avoided.

When I was a young girl, one of my grandmothers' boyfriends molested me. My grandmother would be in the bed with her back turned sleeping. I was about nine or ten years old when I saw this episode of Oprah Winfrey where these sisters were talking about how their dad had molested them, and if I am not mistaken, he was in jail. While watching, I thought to myself maybe something could be done about this man that was messing with me; maybe he would go to jail. That episode gave me the courage to tell my grandmother what her boyfriend was doing to me. I went into the bathroom and practiced how I would tell her for about an hour. Finally, I worked up the nerve. Her response was that I was lying. The next day, she told her boyfriend to stay away from me because I had an active imagination. Before that day, my grandmother and I were close; she spoiled me, and she was my whole world. From the day I told her what her boyfriend had done and well into my twenties, she hated me with a passion. So much so she couldn't stand the sight of me, and often when our family had big get-togethers, especially for the holidays, she would become agitated with me and create a reason to curse me out so bad that I would have to go in a separate room by myself while everyone else was celebrating and visiting. I was often isolated. Sometimes she would even make me leave the house. I didn't realize until years later that she did that because she was afraid that I would tell the family what her boyfriend had done. I had an uncle who said one time that he didn't understand why she acted like this with me, but I knew... I just never said anything until I was grown. It was fear. For some reason, she was deathly afraid that I would tell the family what had happened. Even after the violator was no longer in the picture, she resented me, and her hatred for me lasted until a few years before she passed.

My grandmother was a broken woman who did not know much happiness. She had a hard life, and while that is not an excuse, it is a reason. I was expecting something that she did not have the capacity to give me at the time. For years, I carried hatred and resentment for her because she absolutely broke my heart. I was a child, and I adored my grandmother before all of this happened. She should have protected me, but that was not what hurt me the most. It was her rejection and hatred of me, it was the venom that she spewed on me that ripped me to pieces. As an adult, I didn't come around much because she reminded me of the pain and agony I had suffered at her hand. She had made my life growing up a living hell, and she had never apologized.

My grandmother was something else, and everyone in our family probably got put out or cursed out occasionally by her, but what she did to me was different than what she did to anyone else in the family. The degree and depth of hatred were reserved for me alone. I was paying for her guilt. So it was hard to be around her and act like everything was okay even years later. She had not taken responsibility. I wanted an apology and some acknowledgment that she understood the gravity of what she had done to me...but for years, I got nothing. My pain was real, and I wanted her to put some validity to it.

For years, I remained broken. I tried to forgive, but the righteous indignation that I felt toward her and the situation would not allow me to truly be healed. In the times that my grandmother would launch her attacks on me, she would say things like she wished I was dead and never born. She would say I was worthless, that she hated me. I had been called every name under the sun. I had been told that I was a prostitute and was good-for-nothing. I was told everyone hated me, nobody loved me, and that nobody wanted to be around me. I had heard this from ten years old until I left her house after getting saved and giving my life to Jesus at twenty years old. Ten years of being told you are nothing, I started to believe it, and truth be told, that is why it was difficult to forgive her. It was because I had started to believe what she said about me. I could not stand myself, so I most certainly could not find the love in my heart to forgive her at the time. I thought she owed me an apology, and I thought that if she would just admit what she had done to me, some big weight would be lifted off my shoulder. I thought that would make everything okay. See, I was expecting my grandmother to heal me instead of JESUS. It didn't matter if she never apologized. Jesus's love was powerful enough to comfort and heal me. If I had pressed into God instead of holding out for my "come to Jesus" moment with my grandmother, I would have allowed God's Word to heal me and reveal to me how He saw me.

I was expecting something from her that she didn't have at the time. She didn't have the capacity to ask for forgiveness; she didn't have the ability to accept responsibility; she didn't have the ability to truly be sorry.

Sometimes we are holding out for people to take accountability for their actions, but in doing that, you are holding yourself up also. What if they never say sorry, will you stay bound with an unforgiving and loveless heart toward them? They are obviously broken. So are you going to remain broken with them? Is it worth it? God gets no glory in this, and there is no victory in it. We can't wait for someone to take responsibility before we decide to pursue healing for our souls. We are giving the people power over us that they do not deserve when we refuse to forgive. We give people power when we choose to stay hurt, bound, and broken by what they have done to us. And no matter how you think you are prospering in other areas, if you have not forgiven, you are bound and have given your power away. Hasn't that offense, situation, or person already taken enough from you? Will you allow the enemy to keep taking from you? God forbids. Unforgiveness wears you down. Be free and get up from that broken place. Let go and decide to forgive.

Years later, when I was in my early thirties, my grandmother fell ill. I went to visit her in the hospital, and I could tell she was at the end of her life, and she knew it too. She started to cry and grabbed my hand. She looked at me, and with the little strength she had in her, she said to me, "I am so sorry. Please forgive me." She kept saying it over and over. Here it was, over twenty years later, when she is dying, she apologizes. For years I had imagined what it would feel like for her to acknowledge and be sorry for what she did to me... and here it was, and I felt nothing but sorrow for her. Her apology did not feel like I thought it would. It didn't do what I had always imagined. What I thought I would gain out of hearing her say sorry alluded me.

We wait all this time for something that we think will make the pain go away when really, our healing is in Jesus. Do not wait for an apology. Don't wait on the person to acknowledge and understand that they hurt you. You may never get that, and if you do, it may not make you feel like you think it will. You may have wasted years being angry. Please know, what you are really looking for can only be found in Jesus.

Now, in hindsight, many years later, I wish that I could have pushed past my pain while she was alive and found it in my heart to minister to my grandma. I'd known Jesus for years by this time. Why didn't I purposely go around her to try and make a difference? I lost years and opportunities being unforgiving. While wallowing in my hurt and the injustice of my life, I missed the chance to show her Christ, to show my family Christ. I was too broken. I was too hurt, and I wasted time waiting on an apology when God's power was strong enough to heal me and give me the strength I needed to push past my pain and find an opportunity for God to be glorified. I will never know if I could have effectively ministered to my grandma because I didn't try. Yes, I told her about Jesus and invited her to church and talked to her about God here and there, but I had put more effort into trying to win strangers than I had done with her at that time. God can mend relationships. He can restore, but if we don't give Him the opportunity to do so, we will never know what that feels like.

My grandmother died in my early thirties, and if I am honest, I have to say that I don't know if I truly forgave her until after she passed. I was still dealing with the pain years after she was gone.

We lose so much when we settle in our pain. We lose time, relationships, love, and so much more. We use our pain as an excuse for our dysfunction. We think it is justified, but nothing is further from the truth. God's strength is made perfect in our weakness when you think you can't forgive. If you allow God to help you, He will. Holding grudges cost you more than what you are willing to pay and offers you less than what you think. Matter of fact, you are paying for something to steal from you and cause you destruction. Don't allow unforgiveness to rule in your heart or your life.

Sometimes if we look past what was done to us, we can understand why. We live in a broken world with broken people. Hurt people hurt other people. And remember, you too have been the cause of someone's pain, and at some point, there was a person that had to choose to forgive you. Free yourself and forgive. And if that is all you can do, then that is okay. But if you can forgive and find it in your heart to offer compassion and help to the one that hurt you, well, that takes some supernatural strength, but it is possible. I would suggest, in all things, do what God leads you to do—nothing more and nothing less.

Often, it is the enemy's plan to try and destroy relationships that God has a purpose for. The relationship may be a resource, it may be an encouragement, it may be a piece of the puzzle that is needed for you to fulfill purpose and for them to fulfill purpose. It is meant to bless you, the other party, and others in a way that you can't see right now, so if it is meant to bless and build the kingdom of God, you must know the enemy will do anything he can to try and cause offense and destruction. And because we don't really realize what is going on, we allow the enemy to accomplish exactly what he wanted, and that was to destroy a God-given and purpose-filled relationship.

I have had many relationships that I never thought would be restored. I didn't think I could get past the pain. But God has a way about Him that if you let Him, He will restore a relationship, and it ends up being better than it was before the issue occurred. When we go through something traumatic and a person does something that hurts us, sometimes we only see the offense, we only see what they did. Our vision and memory get skewed. For years when I thought about my grandma, I immediately associated her with evil as if there was nothing good about her. But I realized, after I truly forgave her, I started to miss her. I remembered how funny she was. I wish that I could hang around her one more time and talk and laugh with her, but by the time I had this epiphany, it was too late; she was already gone. I remembered that she could be incredibly tender and sweet. She could be affectionate, and when she was in a good mood, there was nothing that she wouldn't do for you. I found myself wanting to lie across her bed and lie on her leg while talking to her one more time. While she was alive, unforgiveness had caused me to forget all the good things about her. Don't let this be you. Life is too short. Make the most out of what you have left. Hindsight is 20/20. If I knew then what I know now, I would have spent as much time with my grandma as I could. Unforgiveness stole healing that I could have received, time that I could have spent, experiences that could have been created, and triumphs that could have been accomplished by forgiving and allowing the power of God's love to be exemplified. Now, all I can do is pray God uses what I have learned to help others and prevent them from living in unforgiveness. By now, I hope you have grasped that being unforgiving hurts you so much more than the object of your unforgiveness. Unforgiveness prevents healing from taking place. You must forgive so that you can start to heal.

And while you are working on forgiving others for what they have done to you, you need to work on FORGIVING YOURSELF. For some, this is even harder than forgiving others. Listen, it brings no glory to God to try and punish yourself when God is trying to heal you and move you to a place of victory. I am very hard on myself, always have been. So I understand the thought of feeling guilty and ashamed for doing something that you know did not please God. But if you keep living in a state of trying to punish yourself, you are saying that the blood of JESUS and His forgiveness is not powerful enough to forgive whatever it is that you have done. That does not glorify God. Is His death and the blood that He shed for your sins not powerful enough to forgive and cover your sins or your wrong if you have repented? It does not give us any extra notches on our honor belt to punish ourselves when God has forgiven us. Whatever God is going to do as a result of what we have done, He will do. He does not need our help. His Word says that "there is now no condemnation to them that are in Christ Jesus, who walk not after the flesh but after the spirit" (Rom. 8:1). You made a mistake. Repent and accept the forgiveness of God. If you are not living in sin, if you are not continually repeating the same mistake or sin repeatedly with your eyes wide open, then walk in freedom and the liberty that the blood of Jesus and being filled with His spirit affords you. "Stand fast therefore in the liberty where with Christ has made you free, and don't be entangled again with the yoke of bondage" (Galatians 5:1).

Sometimes we erroneously think that being hard on ourselves is a sign of how much we love God and our keen awareness of how we disappointed Him. No, obeying Him and His Word, loving Him, and loving what He loves is a clear indication of our love for Him; and He loves you, so you must also love you. Not forgiving ourselves is just a sign of how we feel about ourselves, and that is something that we must ask God to help us with. This is not to say don't feel sorrowful, broken, or remorse when we disappoint God. Rather, I am saying after you have repented AND asked Him for forgiveness. We have to believe that the God we are asking will do just that. We must have the faith that He is a loving God, a God of His word. We can't doubt Him and think that we still need punishment when He says that He will forgive you. Who knows better: you or God? Forgive yourself. Let go of the anger you have for yourself over that mistake, over that situation, over the wrong decision, over that sin, over the time you wasted. God forgave you; now forgive yourself. LET IT GO.

We have to get to the forgiving part so that we can get to the healing part where we deal with the wreckage that was left behind in our heart and our mind. We can no longer remain stuck; we must move forward so that we can love right, have the right relationships so that we can have peace with God, with ourselves, and with each other. Forgiveness is a must. It is the will of God for your life so that you can be free and so God can use you for His glory. Be free. Forgive them and forgive yourself.

Forgiveness is powerful. Let God's power reign in you!

CHAPTER 10

Pain into Purpose

Have you ever experienced a pain so palpable it felt tangible? Where the mass and weight of it seemed too hard to press through? And since you couldn't press through the pain, you set up shop right in the middle of it and created a home. The pain I am talking about is an emotional pain so severe it causes anguish—the kind of pain where you could feel the tears burn as they filled the depths of your heart. A hurt that took all the wind out of you as the pieces of your soul seemingly broke and shattered within you. **I'm talking about when you thought that pain had done its worse, the bottom fell out and you were introduced to it in a whole new more intimate way.**

Have you ever been in a place where you felt you had nothing else to give? Where every breath caused you pain and the thought of giving in and giving up seemed like the only thing that could bring relief? The thought of putting your foot to the ground caused you anxiety and despair. So you longed to go right back to sleep as soon as you woke up. You couldn't find hope in any of the places you searched for it. You started running on fumes, and then your capacity to maintain relationships, priorities, or anything meaningful started to dissipate. You became emotionally, socially, mentally, physically, and spiritually depleted. This kind of pain seeps into every area of our lives and leaves us vulnerable and more likely to open doors for the enemy! You become isolated and imprisoned to the pain. Right about here is when the enemy starts to claim victory and says, "MISSION ACCOMPLISHED." You fell for it, signed, sealed, delivered. He has drawn you out long enough that if you don't get up from this place, and SOON, your demise is imminent.

DID YOU KNOW THAT THIS IS EXACTLY WHERE THE ENEMY WANTS YOU? After he has sat back and watched your hurt, your pain, and laughed at it, he tries to capitalize on your weakness and bring more pain and destruction before you can come to yourself. He tries to drive your heart, hope, faith, and strength into the ground before you realize that you don't have to be in this place. He bombards your mind with thoughts of delusion, paranoia, and lies to make you feel as if fighting is pointless. He reminds you of the relationship's loss, disappointments, the hurt suffered and perpetrated, the time loss, the regrets, the mistakes, the offenses, the betrayals. He tries to make you feel as if nothing matters, and that nothing can make it right. And even though there are so many scriptures in God's Word to combat all these thoughts and bring you into a place of truth and victory, the enemy is fighting ferociously to cut you off from any life source. So he tries to make you feel as if you do not matter to anyone so that you won't reach out. He tries to make you feel as if you do not have an impact and that your life has been a waste and any effort to pursue freedom and victory is pointless. BUT THIS IS A LIE. Consider the source. And I know, sometimes it is hard to do because we don't realize when it's us or the enemy talking. So we sometimes think that all the negative thoughts about ourselves, our situation, and our lives are coming from us, when in reality, it is the enemy that has been allowed to come in and rent free space in your mind and plant thoughts. The only way to refute, combat, and defeat the enemy is with the truth, which is the Word of God.

IF ONLY YOU KNEW what was on the other side waiting for you. If you would just take your eyes off the pain and put them on JESUS so you can press through! The only way the enemy can wreak havoc on us is if we come from up under the safety of Jesus, if our minds were not fixed on Him, and we were not acknowledging Him in all our ways so that He could direct our path. Somewhere somehow, we took our eyes off the problem solver and put them on the problem. I promise you, there has NEVER BEEN A PERSON WHO LIVED IN THE PRESENCE OF God, whose eyes, mind, and heart were fixed on Jesus, who lost this battle to the enemy. NEVER. For God's Word says that in His (Jesus) presence, there is fullness of joy, and at His right hand, there are pleasures forevermore.

See, one of the things the enemy MUST DO is get you out of the safety and presence of God. He tries to silence your praise, isolate you, get you to stop praying, fasting, meditating on God's Word, and to stop worshipping God. If the enemy can control your thoughts, he can inject your heart with his poisons, and when he gets into your heart, he can dictate your actions, and at that point, you have allowed his influence to be greater than that of God. There is a reason that Jesus told us to guard our hearts for out of it are the issues of life. The only person, place, or thing that should ever sit on the throne of your heart is Jesus. That means He is the center of everything you do, everything you are, and everything that you desire. You put safeguards around your heart, such as hiding His Word in your heart and meditating on it day and night. You guard your heart by being transformed by the renewing of your mind, casting down every imagination and every thought that is contrary to what God says about you and your situation. You reject the thoughts of the enemy and anybody else's thoughts that do not line up with God's Word—even if it's you. You reject every lie that tries to come into your mind. You do not think on it or dwell on it. You immediately cast that thought down and do not receive it into your spirit, and to combat that thought, you rehearse God's Word and think on the things that are good, lovely, true, honest, the things that have and will add virtue, the things that are praiseworthy…and you rehearse the truth in your mind until those negative thoughts are gone and until what you are meditating on in your mind gets into your spirit. You team up with the Holy Spirit against yourself and kick the enemy out of your mind so that he cannot come in and infiltrate your heart.

Jesus is our hiding place. When we hide in Him, the enemy does not stand a chance, and he knows this, so Satan must draw us out. I am not saying you won't experience pain in JESUS because that would be a lie. But what I am saying is that when you are in JESUS, if you stay under the shadow of the Almighty, if you stay in the safety of His will, He can heal you and strengthen you from within, so much so that He can use the hurt that you experienced for good in some way. Whether it be to help others or to help you become more like Him or to just draw you closer to Him…your pain is never wasted if you give it to God. When you go through trials, when your heart is broken, when you are confused, this is the time to run to God. Talk to Him and keep talking to Him until He changes you in the situation, changes the situation, or until He does both. I am telling you, there is a way to get through the pain. I know; I did it. You must set your mind on God and always seek truth. Embrace it and wear it as a cloak, even if the truth hurts you; the truth will make you free. Jesus says that we are to come to Him, all of us that labor and are heavy laden so that He can give us rest. We are to take His yoke upon us because it is light, and it is easy. Give your pain to Jesus; He knows exactly what to do with it, and believe me, He will wield it to work for your good.

Why not give it to Him anyway? He is the only one who can turn that pain into purpose. He is the only one that can heal you so thoroughly that by the time you come out of it, you feel no remnants of the pain—only strength, wisdom, and gratefulness to God for working all things together for your good. What if that pain that He carried you through and that you got the victory over was allowed so that God could use you to help save the lives of others? Jesus died so that we may have life. Are we not willing to die to our flesh so that God can get the glory out of our lives and minister to others who were broken just like we were? See, there is no testimony if there was no test. There would be no need for ministry if there was no misery. There would be no need for a deliverer if there was no need for deliverance. Somebody must be sick in order to be healed. Someone must be broken in order to be made whole. And remember, sin introduced this reality into the world. We cannot blame God because we experience hardships and pain. However, we can seek Him and His will. We can find refuge if we look to Him.

If you have never gone through a pain so devastating as described, I pray you never have to. If you haven't, you may not understand what I am talking about when I say a person can place pain on the throne in their life and it then becomes their Lord and master.

However, there are thousands of people who know all too well what I am talking about, and they too have suffered some sort of heartache and didn't or haven't made it out of their prison of despair. Some went back to the world to double down and dive into the destruction and pain that they could not find a way to escape, and others are still struggling to cope right now and don't know how to come out. Then there are those that came to the most devastating and heart-breaking decision one could make, and that is to end the pain themselves. There are countless people in the grave who died with their purpose unfulfilled. But did you know that this does not have to be you? There is another way. And that is God's way. And this means you must be in a place to hear Him, or if you can't hear Him, just trust Him and His Word.

It's hard to navigate through pain and suffering when there is no understanding of why you must go through it in the first place. And this is where purpose is crucial. If the enemy can prevent you from ever finding out what your purpose is and keep you from finding out who you are in God, then he has won. BUT, if you ever come to yourself and get a revelation of who God is in you, who you are in Him, and the purpose that He has for your life, it is LIGHTS out for the enemy. As long as you are living, there is hope. But tomorrow is not promised. God is ever-present, and He is everywhere. Right now, if you are reading this, and you know you have turned your back on God, or if you are struggling to fight past the pain, I am praying that you come to Him. Call on Him right now. He has all power, He knows where you are, He cares, and He is concerned about you. He is the only one that can heal you. I know you may not see it right now, you may not feel it, but God loves you with a perfect love. His heart is breaking for you as your eyes look upon this page. He is there right now. He has seen how you have self-destructed and tried to numb the pain. He saw you, and His heart broke. Not because He was angry with you, but because you didn't turn to Him. He didn't leave you; He has not forsaken you, and He has not forgotten about you. He loves you with an everlasting love. He has been calling out to you. He has been waiting on you. Will you come to Him? He is the way to your healing. He is the truth that will make you free, and His life that was given in exchange for yours on Calvary has the ability to raise you up from out of this darkness and bring you into His marvelous light of freedom and victory. Aren't you tired of hurting?

It does not matter what it is; Jesus can heal you. It is hard for us sometimes to know how to get out of situations that seem so convoluted, especially when every which way you look you see no escape route, no hope, and no sign of help. BUT JESUS…can make a way of escape if you take it. You don't have to know how; you just have to be willing to forgive whoever and whatever caused the pain and forgive yourself for staying in this place longer than you should have and giving up more than what was required.

See, the Lord says that all things work together for the good to them who love God, to them that are the called according to His purpose. There goes that word again: purpose. Did you know that pain serves a purpose? However, the awareness of purpose is normally only recognized after the process to bring about the manifestation is near the end or complete. Meaning, in your worst heartbreak, or the most difficult trial or time in your life, in the persecution, affliction, famine, desolation, and suffering, we can't see how any good can come out of it. But that is only because the pain won't allow you to see past it. But good is destined to come out of your trial if you love God and if you hold on a little longer. On the other side of this valley of pain is victory. And just because you don't see it does not mean it isn't there. You don't want to give up and give out now. You have come too far; you have been through too much. You might as well press on and see what the end will be. Don't let the enemy take another one out; don't let that be you. There is victory at the end of your story. Let God do what only He can do. One thing is for certain: if you give up and stay in this broken place, you will never come out. If you relinquish and ask the Lord to help you through this, your breakthrough is nigh thee, even if you can't see it naturally.

That is why when we go through pain and any adverse emotion, we need to run to God, not away from Him. We are human with finite understanding and limited sight. We try to understand things far beyond our capacity. But God saw our beginning and is standing at our end, and He knows all things in between. His ways are not our ways; His thoughts are not our thoughts; He is the only sovereign one. His ways are past finding out; why He allows some things are just beyond us. We just need to know He is the author and the finisher of our faith. So although we cannot see how this pain will bring about something beautiful, something powerful, something that can give God glory, it will if you allow Him to finish the work in you that He started. God may or may not have brought the heartache, but He is certainly the only one that can truly free you from it.

There is purpose in the pain. I have never gone through a painful situation that did not eventually work out for my good in the long run. I either learned a lesson and gained wisdom, drew closer to the Lord, became more like Him because the process killed a part of my flesh that was not allowed to go where God was taking me, and/or God used it to help someone else. I do not like pain, and to be honest, I don't know that I would say I welcome it, but if it comes, I know what to do, and that is: turn to Jesus. Press into Him, hide in Him, pray, keep my mind on Him, and if the pain seems too unbearable and I can't muster the strength to speak an audible word, I will cry out in my heart to Him and ask Him for His mercy and grace to deliver me. I ask that His strength be made perfect in my weakness. I let Him know I don't know how to make it through, so I need Him to carry me. I need Him to lead me and cloak me with His love. I ask Him for comfort and for His peace that surpasses all understanding. But I must be willing to put the situation and my heart in His hands.

And to be honest, the only way we will be able to do this is if Jesus helps us and if we do like the scripture says. The Bible talks about the joy that was set before Jesus. And because of this joy, He was able to endure the most horrific and painful thing that has ever been done to a human being. There was no physical pain that any of us could ever experience that was greater than that of what Jesus went through. And there was no emotional, mental, spiritual pain greater than that of Jesus being lied on, persecuted, afflicted, betrayed, forsaken, rejected, and crucified by those He created and came to die for so that they can be reconciled back to Him. It is so unjust and so far beyond what we go through because He didn't deserve any of it. He was perfect in every way. Everything He ever suffered was for us. Our light affliction, which is temporary, works a far more exceeding an eternal weight of glory in us. No matter what we have gone through, it cannot be compared to what Jesus went through. God gave His only begotten Son. He put on flesh and came down here to redeem us Himself.

On all accounts, Jesus had it worse than any other human being who ever lived or who will ever live. And because He focused on purpose being fulfilled, He endured the cross. He endured the pain, He endured the nails in His hands, the nails in His foot, the crown of thorns on His head, the cattle nine tail whippings, and with every lash and every pain felt, He thought of you and rejoiced. For the joy that was set before Him, He endured the cross. As the flesh was ripped from His body, He thought of you. He did not focus on the pain, but He kept His mind on purpose, and the manifestation of that purpose is you. The joy of seeing you set free, healed, and delivered. The joy of having a relationship with you. He loved us that much. If any of us were there when this was happening, we probably would have seen it the same way we see our situations today when we are going through. It sounds devastating and painstaking to think that Jesus was beaten, battered, and bruised. If you were in the crowd when the people were cheering for a murderer to go free rather than the one who came to save them, I am sure we would have thought the situation was bleak, hopeless, and unredeemable. We wouldn't have known the end of the story because we could have only seen what we saw at the time unless God gave us insight. We wouldn't have known that Jesus dying on the cross wasn't the end of the story. Likewise, with our own situations, we sometimes focus on what we see and feel now, rather than the joy that is set before us. And we don't focus on the joy set before us because a lot of us don't know what that joy is. For Jesus, the purpose in the pain was the ability to offer salvation to His creation; it was restored fellowship and communion, it was receiving power and victory over death and being able to offer that to us through Him. His pain was unimaginable, yet it brought God the greatest glory that has ever been wrought. Everybody thought Jesus was dead, never to be seen again. But He rose, and when He arose, He did it with all power.

The servant is not greater than his master. Can God get the glory out of your life? If you will endure and persevere, there is a resurrection of power waiting on the other side of this test. You will come out stronger and wiser.

There is a scripture in the Bible that says, "That I might know Him, and the power of His resurrection and the fellowshipping of His sufferings, being made conformable unto His death" (Phil. 3:10). How will you come to know Him? I would suggest it is in the fellowshipping of His sufferings, and it is in that fellowship, that like or shared experience, that you will start to be conformed unto His death. What does that really mean? The act of being made conformable unto His death is the process in which you become dead to anything that would keep you from Jesus or keep you from following His example.

If there is nothing else that will ever come out of this life, if there is nothing else that I will ever gain by going through trials, tribulation, disappointment, heartbreak, famine, and pain other than being able to be with Jesus for all eternity, then it is well worth it. The devil would like to trick us into suffering hell down here on earth and then going to hell for all eternity because we did not put our hope, faith, and trust in God. If I suffer down here and am unable to endure and turn my back on God, how will I endure an eternity in hell? We must keep the JOY of being with Jesus ever set before us. We are living to live again. This life is temporal, but the one after this is for eternity. We must get anchored in God; that is the only way that pain, death, or any other thing won't be able to separate us from Him. Our minds have to be made up that no matter what comes, and no matter what goes, whether that be every single relationship we have, every penny we have, every bit of influence we have, our health, the loss of businesses, the loss of loved ones, reputations, or all the above. If we are anchored in Jesus, nothing will be able to tear us apart from Him. If we keep our eyes on the prize which is JESUS, we can make it. It is hard, but we can do it. And if that is the only reward for enduring the suffering, then that is more than the whole world. However, God is such a loving God. He is such a sovereign and amazing Lord, almost always—there is more to the story than this—although that is enough.

There is a scripture, in Romans 8:35–39, that says, "Who shall separate us from the love of Christ? shall, tribulation, or distress, or persecution, or famine, or nakedness, or peril or sword? As it is written, for thy sake we are killed all the day long; we are accounted as sheep for the slaughter. Nay in all these things we are more than conquerors through him that loved us. For I am persuaded, that neither death, nor life, nor angels, nor principalities, nor powers, nor things present, nor things to come, nor height, nor depth, nor any other creature, shall be able to separate us from the love of God which is in Christ Jesus our Lord."

God dealt with me about this scripture some years ago, and it has helped me get through some of the most horrific times in my life. What I come to understand is that going through all these things should only bring us closer to Jesus if we really love Him like we say we do. For instance, after going through tribulation, I realized that eventually, I began to learn to trust the Lord. After a few times of seeing that inevitably Jesus comes through, it may not be when I want Him to but that it is always on time it caused me to start going through tribulation with a little more trust in Him and ease. If you love God and you lean into Him when you experience distress, you will come to see that somehow, miraculously, you begin developing a peace that could only come from Him. You realize that the persecution worked pride and judgment out of you, and in exchange, you gained humility and compassion. In experiencing lack and famine, it causes you to develop an insatiable desperation for God. There is nothing that shall be able to separate us from the love of Christ. Matter of fact, in suffering and enduring these things, it should draw us closer to Jesus if we love Him, and this confounds the enemy. When we flip the script on our pain, and instead of being a victim of it, we become the victor—that is the power of resurrection being exemplified in our life.

Whatever your pain stems from, in the grand scheme of things, it is inconsequential—because God can heal you. At the end of the day, we are at war, whether we know it or not. If you acknowledge it or if you don't, the fact remains that the devil is trying to use pain to kill, steal, and destroy you. However, God allows these same things that the devil would use to destroy to purify you. He uses it to kill your flesh and everything in you that is not like Him, and then He brings you out so that He may be glorified and that you may then go and help others which glorifies Him even the more. Then on top of that, He will bless and reward you for doing what is best for you to do anyway. He will bless you for choosing healing and peace. You get to choose the outcome by how you respond to the pain. If I am being honest, I don't know that I would love Jesus as deeply as I do or appreciate Him nearly as much if I hadn't been broken. It is a broken and contrite spirit that God will not despise. He will come to your rescue if you let Him.

Once we come out of our trial with victory, Jesus uses it for His glory. Just like He loves you, He loves others that are in the same situation that you used to be in. They are hurting, even right now. There are people that are in a very dark place. Most of them, you wouldn't even know it because they smile and joke around. Pain has many different faces. It doesn't always look like what it is. Would you be surprised to learn that those smiles and jokes are sometimes a smoke screen? Sometimes it is the people that seem like they have everything all together, but they are often the ones that are battling and suffering in silence the most. Did you know that some of the people that seem strong, the ones that you look to for help and guidance, are broken themselves? And after they get done telling everybody else how to trust in Jesus, how to endure, and look to Him for strength, they themselves are fading away. There are people in our family, at our job, in our church, people that we encounter on an everyday basis who are waiting on us. But we are looking at our pain, and not the God over the pain. Look to the one who has all power. Set the joy of being with Him, of pleasing Him, of knowing that He wants to use you for His glory ever before you. Focus on that when you are going through. If you knew that your life could save a life, would you allow God to use you? Let God turn your misery into your ministry. This thought has driven me and pulled me through. I set my mind on two things, and that was making it to heaven to be with Jesus for all eternity and to fulfill His will down here on the earth. Don't let your pain be in vain.

Let Him pour you out on the broken so that they may be healed through your victory and through your testimony. This is the will of God. There is victory waiting for you. There is truly purpose in the pain.

CHAPTER 11

I'm Dying to Love You

Imagine the Lord giving insight into every relationship you have had and ever will have. What if He allowed you to see the beginning of those relationships? Along with how they would develop, and how they would all play out. If you could know the end result of a relationship before you went into it, would you want to? What if you learned that the relationship would only bring heartache? What if you learned that some of those relationships would involve betrayal? Now let's add another layer to the equation. What if in all these relationships, you were loving, giving, sacrificing, long-suffering, and everything that a good friend—mate, family member, or business partner—would be, but you were repaid with non-appreciation, ungratefulness, abuse, rejection, deceit, and so on. Would you choose to still entertain these relationships if you had a choice to avoid them altogether, given that you are aware of the outcome? Most of us would probably choose to forgo the relationships that caused hurt, damage, and what we think to be wasted time.

Now let's take this a step further. What if one of the same people who severely mistreated you, lied on you, tarnished your reputation, and tried everything that they could to make your life miserable now needed your help in some way. Most of us would like to "think" we would help hands down. But would we really? What if what they needed from us was something we would only do for family or for someone close to us, but we were the only one who could do it for them? Guess what? This is exactly what Jesus did. He knew the beginning from the end. He knew that some of us would reject Him, abuse His grace and mercy, be ungrateful, non-appreciative, unloving, and unforgiving. He knew the outcome before He went into it, and with that knowledge, He looked at you and me and decided to die for us anyway. Jesus gave His life for those that wanted Him crucified. Those that murdered Him, He died for—the Creator being persecuted by His own creation and still choosing to provide a way for them to be redeemed.

"For as by one man's disobedience many were made sinners, so also by one man's obedience, many will be made righteous" (Romans 5:19). In Adam we die; in Christ, we live. Because of the fall of Adam, we were born into a fallen world. The Bible describes it as being shaped in iniquity. We were born into sin, and the penalty for sin is death, which is why Jesus took our place on the cross and died for our sins. He wanted to restore the fellowship that once existed between Him and His creation. He wanted to provide redemption and salvation for all who would seek it.

Jesus knew that there was no greater demonstration of love and no greater act of sacrifice than dying for those whom He loved. The Bible says in John 3:16 that, "For God so loved the world that He gave his only begotten son, that whosoever believeth in him should not perish but have everlasting life." This verse is very insightful as it relates to the love of

God. See, the scripture states that God so loved the world, and because He so loved the world, there was something that He gave (sacrificed) which was His only begotten Son, but then it goes on to give the reason why (purpose) He did the aforementioned so that whoever believed in Jesus would not perish but have everlasting life. There was a purpose—something He wanted to accomplish. To fulfill this purpose, it took the greatest act of love that man has ever known. Jesus's crucifixion was the worst pain that has ever been suffered, but it brought about the greatest glory ever revealed culminating with His resurrection.

Sometimes we question God's love for us, but what He did on the cross for us should answer every doubt we have. He knew that we were sinners; He knew that we would be disobedient; He knew that we were liars, whoremongers, backbiters, murderers, and so on. It does not matter what you have done, or how horrendous it was. His blood that was shed paid the price for it. Even the most horrible of sins that we may find it hard to forgive others for, the love of Jesus paid for that sin with His faultless, sinless, and powerful blood. There is no place that you can go physically, mentally, emotionally, or spiritually where God is not there. Knowing everything that can be known about us, He chose to give His life. The only thing we must do to receive His gift of salvation is to believe in Him and follow His steps for salvation as outlined in Scripture.

Jesus loves us with an everlasting love. He showed us a love so powerful that it conquered death. And if we have the Spirit of God living on the inside of us, then we are to love as Jesus loved. He says this in John 15:12–13: "This is my commandment, that ye love one another AS I HAVE LOVED YOU." He tells us that we need to love others as He has loved us, and just in case we forgot what that looked like, or just in case we don't know how He loved us, He reminds us. He goes on to say in that same scripture: "Greater love hath no man than this, that a man lay down his life for his friends." So let us ponder. Is Jesus saying that we should lay down our lives for our friend? Are we to die and be crucified like Christ?

The Bible says in 1 John 3:16 that "we know that we have passed from death to life if we love the brethren." What does all of this mean, and what am I trying to say? Glad you asked.

This book is to offer revelation when God gives it or a different perspective and way of looking at things, and both when applicable. For the context in this book, I am not saying Jesus is requiring us to die a physical death for others. However, what is being introduced is the thought of dying to our flesh daily so that the love of God can be revealed in and through us. It is clearly outlined in the scriptures above that Jesus is requiring us to love as He has loved. It is also clearly outlined in the scriptures exactly how He loved. He laid down His life. Why did He do that? So that purpose could be fulfilled.

Hebrews 12:2 talks about how "For the joy that was set before Jesus, he endured the cross, despising the shame, and is set down at the right hand of the throne of God." What was that joy that was set before Him that allowed Him to endure the greatest suffering ever experienced? It was the joy of seeing us reconciled back to Himself, the joy of us receiving eternal life if we receive Him, the joy of us once again fellowshipping with Him, and for His purpose to be fulfilled in and through us. Likewise, we are to follow this example.

For the joy that is set before us (eternal life, pleasing God, and His will being fulfilled in us and through us), we are to endure the cross of persecution, affliction, hurt feelings, famine, suffering, or whatever our cross is so that God's purpose may be fulfilled through us. God wants to use us as an extension of Himself so that His will may be fulfilled on the earth. And the dying part comes in when we must die to everything that would prevent the powerful life-giving love of Jesus from being able to flow through us freely with no restrictions.

See, while God died for us knowing that we were no good and knowing that not everyone would accept Him, He still chose to give His life for ours. However, we are not too keen on dying to our flesh just so we can love someone the way that God has loved us. We say we love, but do we really know what that means? Do we love when it is easy and draw the line when it gets hard? Sometimes we won't even willingly engage or walk through a difficult situation or relationship if it is going to cause us to suffer in some way, especially if we know it upfront. But what if that suffering is for the glory of God? What if you dying to your flesh and enduring someone that may get on your nerves, or enduring someone you may not understand, or even being long-suffering with someone who may have disappointed or hurt you would fulfill purpose? What if God wants to use you to get them to a place of victory in their life? What if God wants to use you to bring some sort of healing and deliverance in their life, but in order to do so, you may experience a few hardships, hurt feelings, misunderstandings, etc.? Would you die to your flesh so that someone else could live?

We can't see the full picture as He can. We only see in bits and parts. We look at an incomplete picture and try to fill in the blanks. But God knows all things. He is sovereign. Maybe there is a reason the Lord doesn't always reveal to us every single detail. Maybe it's because if we knew we would have to go through something that was painful to bring about purpose, we may choose a different option. Some of us, if not all, would choose to take the path of least resistance. We would take the road that doesn't challenge us. But with no challenges, there is no victory, and with no suffering, there is no glory.

This next thought is to challenge your thinking and perspective.

When the Bible speaks of us knowing that we have passed from death to life, that can only be done through the cross (figuratively speaking). We all have one to bear. Jesus tells us to take up our cross and follow Him. Follow Him where? On the journey of passing from death to life. Jesus went to the cross, and we must go to the cross also. And what happens at the cross? You die. The sign that we have gone to the cross, and that our flesh is dead, and that we have passed from death, and that the love of Christ is now resurrected and living in us is that we are able to love our brethren. And love them how? Again, He tells us…as He has loved us. And how did He love us? He laid His life down for us. If His spirit is in us, then we have the same spirit that was resurrected from the grave. We have the same spirit that defeated death living in us. We have that same spirit that because of the joy that was set before Jesus, He was able to endure the cross and despise the shame. Surely, we can endure hardness as a good soldier and die to our flesh so that the love of God can be demonstrated in us and through us for His glory, right? If we haven't been to that cross yet…we abide in death.

At some point, we must graduate from milk to meat. At some point, we need to be able to handle those things in the Word that challenge us beyond our comfortability and beyond our finite thinking. There was an intended purpose which motivated the display of Jesus's love. Likewise, we must keep the purpose ever before us. This life is not about us. It is about Jesus and His will being fulfilled in us. We need to align our will with His because at the end of the day, only what we do for Christ is going to last.

With that thought in mind, we are to present our bodies a living sacrifice, holy and acceptable unto God which is our reasonable service. God is to be exalted in us, and when we present our bodies as a sacrifice, a willing vessel, a vessel of holiness to be used by God, He, in turn, is glorified. He is seen in us, and His mercy and His love flow through us. And therefore, we must die to love others.

Again, this does not speak of literal physical death, but rather, a death of our flesh, death to everything that would prevent God from being able to really move through us as He pleases. It means death to anything in us that would dishonor God. If pride is keeping you from loving others right, that is something that needs to die on the cross. If unforgiveness is keeping you from allowing God's perfect will to be done through you, then you are holding up God's purpose from being fulfilled, you are being disobedient, and on top of all of that, we are not allowing the glory of God to be revealed through us. If it is pain, or whatever is keeping us from loving like Jesus loved us, it needs to die so that the love of Christ can abound and live in and through us.

Remember, this is about Jesus and Him being glorified. Jesus, willingly, fully knowing the extent to which He would suffer, chose to do so anyway. He surrendered to the purpose and will for His life, and did not seek revenge or administer judgment, although it was in His power to do so. He kept the main thing the main thing. And what was that? It was the joy of you and I being able to receive eternal life. Jesus sacrificed and restrained Himself from fighting His own battles. He even stopped Peter from trying to fight the battle for Him. Why? Because up ahead, He saw you and me, and He knew that we would need a Redeemer. He knew that we would not be able to handle the penalty of death that we deserved. **His passion pushed through the pain so that purpose could be fulfilled. That is love. Can we do the same?** Can we push through the pain so that purpose can be fulfilled in us and through us? Can we suffer humiliation, rejection, persecution, affliction, a tarnished reputation, and betrayal so that God's glory can be manifested? Yes, we can, but the better question is: would we? Can we suffer a little while if God would eventually show forth His glory through your situation?

It's not hard to love those who we always seem to agree with, those with whom we have had no issues. That is easy, but really...where is the glory in that? Not to say it isn't a good thing, but we should be asking ourselves, can we love when things are hard? When things are difficult? Can we love when we are not getting along? Can we love when someone is not our cup of tea? We have accepted a watered-down version of what love is, and this is why often there is no power being manifested through our relationships. We only cultivate and nurture our relationships to the extent of our comfort, to our own limit, and when it goes past our boundaries or our idea of how it should be, or if loving someone challenges us in some way, we remove or distance ourselves. Where is the power to love through the difficulty? Where is the love that will see past what is, and see what will be, and be willing to die for the joy that is set before us? Who can suffer hardness as a good soldier without allowing their heart to turn to stone? Who can show forth the life-giving, life-resurrecting power of love without building fortresses around our heart and systems designed to only allow in the people of our choosing? Who can allow the scripture that says we are accounted as sheep for the slaughter all day long to become alive in our life? Who will be a living sacrifice and a living example of the love of God? Who will pass from death to life by dying to our flesh and coming out on the other side of that cross, loving God's people with a love so powerful that it brings hope, joy, encouragement, deliverance, healing, and set people free? A love so pure and powerful that it will die to whatever hinders it from allowing the love of God to be glorified.

For all intents and purposes, this whole chapter is referring to dying to your flesh so that the love of God can be manifested. To give a balanced perspective, if anyone in your life is killing your spirit, distance yourself and seek direction from God. In this chapter, I am only referring to when people would cause you to have to die to your flesh in order to love them—things such as your opinions, your ill-informed judgments, pride, backbiting, impatience, hardness, insecurity, stubbornness, sensitivity, and so on. What we sometimes miss is that God is doing a multitude of things in one act or situation. You may have a relationship that is testing your patience and revealing your pride, and while God wants you to die to your flesh so that you can love your brother and sister right, the part we miss is that He is also allowing these things to be revealed through this situation so that you can work on you. It is not only for the other person; you are also dying to your flesh so that you can love God more perfectly.

From here on out, let's be more mindful of how we love. We need to pay attention to ourselves, what triggers us to want to retreat from a person or situation. Then ask yourself if it is something in your flesh that causes you to retreat or respond a certain way other than in love. If yes, now you know what needs to die.

So what does this process of dying to our flesh looks like? Spiritually, the best way to approach this is to feed your spirit constantly. Constantly read and study the Word of God, meditate on it, hide it in your heart, pray, fast, consecrate, and spend quality time with the Lord. The more you feed your spirit, the stronger it will become, thus rendering your flesh less and less powerful. Practically, dying to your flesh looks like you, making a conscious and purposeful effort to control your actions and reactions. For instance, if you are dealing with a situation where you know God wants to be glorified, you know a blessing can come out of it. You must know the enemy will try to thwart the purpose of God from being fulfilled, so you can bet that the enemy is raging and causing all kinds of havoc. Do not fall into his trap. If he is trying to cause division, confusion, and chaos, make a concerted effort to think before you react. Don't respond with emotion. See it for what it is. Confound the enemy and allow your spirit to lead. Pray about what is going on, and ask God how to handle it. This may cause you to have to die to your flesh because you may want to go off, you may want to react, you may want to put a person in their place (justified or not), but that is not what God wants because it could be counterproductive to any progress made toward His purpose. So it may require you to die to your need to say something. Can you do this?

For the joy that is set before you, can you endure the cross? It doesn't feel good, but oh, is it glorious to be used by the Lord. Dying to our flesh may also look like being unjustly persecuted for righteousness' sake. Do we fight back in our flesh, or do we pass from death to life and die to our will so that God's will can be done through us and so that He can be glorified and shine through us? If we are going to really love like Jesus, at some point, we must make a visit to that cross—something has got to die. Too often have we patted ourselves on the back, tooting that our love walk is perfect when it hasn't even been challenged. Some of us have experienced some sort of death when having to love our family members back to life, but even then…it's our family. I do not believe God made a distinction in the Bible when He was talking about love. He did not only lay down His life for His immediate family members or those who He deemed worthy of His sacrifice of love. None of us were worthy, and He died for us all. He did not say you know you have passed from death to life when you have loved your family and those who are easy to love. He said you know when you love the brethren.

Can we look at the test, the trial, the persecution, the pain, the hardship that we are facing and say, "For the joy that is set before me, for the joy of seeing God's purpose fulfilled in this situation, in this relationship, in my brother or sisters life, and in my life, I will endure this cross"? We were commanded to love one another as He (JESUS) loved us. There is no way around it; Jesus gave His life for us. He went to the cross for us. He passed through death unto life with the keys to death when He was resurrected and then sent that same spirit back for us to receive so that we could do the same. We can have power over death if we travel to that cross and crucify our flesh so that the love of God can rule and reign in our hearts.

We need to die to our flesh daily that we may love God more perfectly so that we can love ourselves and others more powerfully. Can God get the glory out of you?

"I'M DYING TO LOVE YOU."

Will you do the same?

CHAPTER 12

Die Empty

There was a time when I was at a crossroad in my life. It got to a point where nothing I did was satisfying. I could no longer pour excuses on top of the purpose that was trying to break through. I knew what I needed to do, but the strength and faith to do it was something altogether different. See, I needed to pursue God with everything I had in me. I needed to cast down the imaginations and all those thoughts that I had exalted high above the thoughts God had of me. I needed to fight through the years of disappointment, rejection, failure, mistakes, and wasted time. I had to acquire the spiritual discipline and intensity that I once had that I let diminish through the weariness and spiritual fatigue that a life of hardships can cause.

Ultimately, I needed to make a decision. Would I let the anointing and call on my life lay waste and in ruins? Would I remain defeated? Or did I want to be all that God called me to be? I had to ask myself, was I really going to lay down and die with purpose unfulfilled, or would I finally stand up and decide to die empty? Would I finally submit totally and completely to God's will so that He could use me for His glory and use me to heal, deliver, and set captives free? Well, as you read this book, you can see... I chose the latter.

With all that is going on in this world, one thing is for sure: Jesus is soon to come. Even as I begin to write this, I feel like crying and repenting. Let me tell you why. Matthew 25:14–30 explains it all.

In this scripture, Jesus likens the kingdom of God as a man traveling into a faraway country who gave his goods to his servants. He gave one servant five talents, the other two, and another one. Over the process of time, while awaiting their master to come back, the servant with the five traded the talents his master gave him and gained five more, and likewise with the one that had two. However, the servant with the one talent buried what his master gave him (he buried his gift, he buried his business, he buried his calling, he buried his anointing, and he buried his ministry). Upon the master's return, the servants had to give an account for what they did with what their master had left with them.

The servant with the five talents told his master that in addition to what was given to him, he gained five more. The servant with the two talents also had a good report to give his master as he had also gained two talents to add to what was entrusted to him. The master was well pleased; he called them faithful, and because they were productive, he gave them even more to MANAGE. Oh, but the servant with the one talent! When it was his turn to explain what he had done with what the master left in his care, he said that he buried it because he was scared. He gave the excuse that his master was a hard man who reaped where he had not sown and gathered where he had not strawed. The master was not pleased. The servant confessed out of his own mouth that he knew the master was going to expect him to build on, be productive with, and add to what was given to him…and even with this knowledge, he still CHOSE to bury the one talent and be unproductive. The master called him wicked (evil) and slothful (lazy, unprofitable), took the one talent he did have and gave it to the one who now had ten (the productive servant), and then cast the evil and slothful servant into outer darkness.

Hmm, I wonder…can WE GO TO HELL for burying and sitting down on the talents (calling, anointing, gifts, purpose) that God has given us? The unprofitable servant in the parable did.

I wondered what made the servant in this parable evil. I could understand calling him lazy or slothful, but what made him evil? So much so that he was cast into outer darkness just for being unproductive. Then the story about the fig tree came to mind.

Now here is Jesus…the Creator of the heavens and earth, the one who made the fig tree and determined its purpose. He is now hungry and comes to reap a fig from the tree, only to discover there was none, and He cursed it. Why? The scripture clearly stated that it was not the season for figs. So Jesus, if you know it is not my season, how can you expect something from me that "I" am not ready to give?

Herein lies the reason (I believe) the tree was cursed, and the servant was called evil. The fig tree had everything it needed to produce; if it didn't, Jesus wouldn't have asked anything of it. Never mind it not being the season for the fig tree to yield fruit; **when Jesus showed up, it became the right season**. In the presence of Jesus, and the fact that He required fruit from the fig tree meant that the tree was no longer under the natural process of time constraints or climate conditions. When the one who created and controls time, seasons, and climates requires something of its creation, the only appropriate and right response is to yield what is asked for. Anything else is disobedience and rebellion. The fig tree, like the servant with the one talent, should have submitted to the will of GOD and gave Him what He required instead of refusing, regardless of what normal circumstances would suggest. Jesus was saying there was no excuse. Likewise, with the evil servant. He was considered evil because he did not do what was expected of him. The master gave all of them talents; obviously he knew what they could handle, which is why he decided to give one five, another two, and the other one. He gave according to their ability (my take). So the servant with the one talent had the ability to gain another talent on top of the one he had but HE chose not to. This shows either a lack of faith or blatant disobedience, but I would venture to say both. The Lord wants a return on the investment that He has given us. That return is the fact that the gift, talent, assignment, call, anointing, etc. benefited someone in addition to yourself in some sort of way that brought the Lord glory and fulfilled His purpose for giving it to you in the first place.

Just like the parable of the talents and the incident with Jesus and the fig tree, God has given us talents, gifts, anointing, purpose, and ability. He is expecting us to manage what He gave us responsibly. We are to do what He wants us to do with them, not what we want or what we feel like or don't feel like doing with them. It does not matter if He gave you five, two, or one talent. He gave it according to the ability HE enabled you to have. So He knows what you are capable of. We do not have a right to bury our talents because we are not ready, because we feel insufficient, because we got hurt in the church, because we are afraid to step out on faith, because we suffered a loss, because we got divorced, because we lost our job, because we don't have the money to do it, because someone discouraged us, because we are scared of what people will say, because we are scared to succeed, or whatever else you can think of. There is no reason, no excuse, and no justification for not giving out all that GOD put in us to use for His glory. If God is requiring it of you, please know that He has already factored in everything you need to produce and fulfill the call and purpose of your life.

If we want to please the Lord, then being who He called us to be, and developing the gifts and talents that He gave us so that it can aid in the ministry that He has entrusted us with is essential. It is nonnegotiable; do not think you have an option on whether you are going to allow GOD to use what He put in you for His glory. If you are submitted to the Lord and want to be used by Him, then the only option is to present our bodies a living sacrifice unto God. So…no, ma'am and no, sir, we DO NOT HAVE THAT OPTION—not if we want to please God.

Whatever it is that God has placed inside of you, be it a talent, a gift, a calling, an anointing, a ministry, your purpose, destiny, or what have you, it is all critically essential to the body of Christ. It must be developed, cultivated, and then used to not only help ourselves but others. It is all for the kingdom and glory of GOD. If the only talent you have is to give hugs because they heal the heart, you had better get to hugging. We have to get over our insecurities, and our fear of—if people will receive us or not. If God gave you the talent to sing, it is not up to you to use that as YOU WILL. It has to be submitted to GOD and then used the way He sees fit… and you don't get the choice of not using it because you do not feel like it or because you refuse to do what is necessary to sharpen your skill. Again, not if you want to please God. If He gave you the ability to start a business, then learn all you can, and do what is necessary so you can do what God has gifted you to do. If God has gifted you to serve, administrate, minister, etc., get in position to use your talent and your gift because if you don't, you will be held accountable.

It is EVIL (undisciplined, egregious, vial, dishonorable) to not produce when the Master producer lives in us. It is evil to not be productive and sit down on what GOD intended us to use for His glory. When we refuse to use what GOD has given us, we put ourselves in the place of God. It's a slap in the face of Jesus—as if we know better than Him. The gifts and the talents are not ours; they belong to Him, and it is up to HIM to tell us what to do with it. If we are not giving Him glory, then what are we living for? If purpose is not being fulfilled in our lives, we are good for nothing. That is just like the fig tree that did not produce fruit for Jesus (when He required it, not when it was ready). It defeats the whole reason for us existing if we do not fulfill the purpose in which GOD created us for.

It is time for us to be used by God in every way He intended. It is time for us to give our all for His glory. It is time to pour out what has been poured in us for so many years. We need to rebuke fear, procrastination, distraction, doubt, interference, demonic attacks, laziness, slothfulness, faithlessness, etc. and allow GOD to stand up in us, stretch out, and get out everything He put in us with nothing lack-ing—FOR HIS GLORY!

One of our greatest fears should be to die with God's unfulfilled purpose still on the inside of us. Who wants to die and everything that they should have been and everything that they should have done dies with them? Is our life a total waste if God created us for a purpose and that purpose goes unfulfilled? What are we waiting on? Who are we waiting for? What if you never get the support and never acquire the resources you feel you need to step out and walk by faith? If you know all the steps and have everything necessary, is that faith? What if you never come to the understanding that you will never be worthy enough in and of yourself, but God chose you anyhow, will that low self-esteem or lack of confidence be an excuse, or will that be the very thing that testifies against you?

If God dwells in us, the God who is sovereign and all-powerful, is that not enough to conquer any and every obstacle that we are faced with? If we allow fear, pain, disappointment, rejection, shame, tribulation, low self-esteem, unforgiveness, or what have you to keep us from doing and becoming all that God called us to be, does that mean that we give more credence and power to the hindrances than to the God who has the power to help us overcome them all?

It is imperative that we get over ourselves so that God can be glorified. The glory is not in us; the glory is in the GOD that is in us, and if we start to look at it that way, it should help our perspective. If you are wondering why God would choose to use you for something that is out of your comfort zone, or why He would use you to do something that you believe you are not qualified to do, then you are missing the point and looking at the situation all wrong. The harder it would be to believe that God can do it through you, the more glory it brings to God when He does exactly that.

The Lord needs vessels that He can shine through, vessels that He can get the glory out of. He knows what each vessel will render. The degree in which you are willing to submit and humble yourself often is the degree in which the Lord will use you. He doesn't necessarily need your ability, your education, your finances, your looks, your reputation, or physique; He needs your willingness to submit a surrendered vessel to

Him. Matter of fact, I believe the Lord takes pleasure in using some of the unlikeliest of people. Again, the more difficult it would be to believe that God would use you in such a way, the greater the glory it brings to the Lord. If people think that you would be the last person that God would use to do what He called you to do, then you could possibly be the greatest candidate for the job. This is because if God does it through you, then people would have no choice but to know that it is God that did it, and not you, and that's what we want. We want GOD to get the glory.

Who would think that a man with speech problems would be used to declare what the Lord said and ultimately, set a whole nation free? Yet God used Moses to do just that. Who would have thought that the man who was beaten, crucified, and treated worse than criminals who committed the most heinous of acts, would actually be the son of God who was sent to be a deliverer to the very people that chose to crucify Him and who were totally oblivious to who He really was? Jesus did not look the part; He was not what they would have chosen for a king. They misjudged Him. That was intentional though. God smuggled eternal life in the earth through Jesus Christ. But Satan played right into the plan of God by using the people whose hearts were evil to crucify Jesus.

Just like Jesus, when you were born, there was something smuggled in the earth through you. Your life may not have been ideal, or storybook, or what one would think for what God called you to be, but that was purposeful. It wouldn't seem likely that a person who was despised and who experienced so much pain, rejection, and persecution would be chosen to one day deliver the very same people that caused the pain. Well, it happened to Joseph. It doesn't seem like there would be much worth in a hotheaded youngster with cowardly tendencies, but Jesus gave Peter the keys to the kingdom. Gideon didn't feel as if he was much of anything, yet God called him a mighty man of valor. You are what God says you are. Will you believe it?

Your life and what you have been through are optics—just a piece of the puzzle. Sometimes the valleys, the tribulations, the inadequacies are a smoke screen to disguise what you are carrying on the inside. See, if you don't look the part, if you don't seem qualified for the part, and if your personality doesn't seem to fit the bill, then the enemy may direct his attention to those who scream aloud that they are something they really are not—all the while…it is YOU that is chosen. Someone is just serving as a placeholder. It is YOU, you are the chosen one. Consider what happened when Samuel went to anoint David. Jesse presented every son he had except David. All of David's brothers looked the part, but the Lord said that none of them were who He had chosen. He reminded Samuel that humans look on the outward appearance but that He looks at the heart. He asked Jesse if he had any other sons, and indeed he did. It was the son who did not look the part, the little shepherd boy who was out with the herd, the one who did not fit the bill, but who was being prepared for it for his whole life. It was him who God had chosen. **The Lord is speaking to someone right now. You don't have to wonder; He is speaking to YOU!**

Some of the things you are perplexed about, God allowed to confuse the enemy, to get the heat off of you and divert the enemy's attention in another direction while God was developing you. What if the Lord was throwing the enemy off your scent to confuse your opposers, so by the time they figure out that GOD hid an anointing to destroy the kingdom of hell inside of you, it is too late for them or the enemy to do anything about it? It's too late now. You have been molded and made ready to walk into that anointing. You have been through the fire, and you are still here, still seeking, still searching, still serving and loving God. The enemy has fought relentlessly to keep you from realizing who you are in God and has fought even harder for you to not BE who God has called you to be. But that ends now. **It's time to flip the script and allow what was once your misery to thrust you into your ministry!**

Get your eyes, mind, and heart off what you are not, and instead, allow God to show you what you ARE and whose you are, and who HE IS IN YOU. Take your eyes off what you cannot do, and put them on what God CAN DO, and then know that He CAN, and He WILL DO IT THROUGH YOU!

Ask God to give you that zeal back, to stir up that passion, to increase that boldness, to strengthen your faith, and GO FOR IT! Take a leap of faith and begin to flap those spiritual wings so that they may gain strength. Take that first step, then take another. Intentionally get out of your comfort zone; intentionally go back to the place that the Lord spoke to you. Pick up every word He gave that you let fall to the ground. Dig up every promise of God that you buried, and ask Him to breathe on it again. Ask Him to shake you again and stir up the gift that is within you. Ask Him to give you an insatiable desire to fulfill the purpose and call on your life. Rebuke fear, and do it scared until the confidence of who God is in you stands up and soars! Empty yourself of everything God put in you. It's not just for you, but it is to help your family, friends, your community, your nation, and the world. What if you became courageous and trusted GOD and allowed Him to use you for His glory to the utmost with nothing lacking?

At the end of the day…only what we DO for Christ will last. Faith without works is dead. The grave is full of good-intentioned people who never materialized those intentions. When it is all said and done, "could've," "should've," "would've," will not cut it and will not serve as a justifiable excuse for not producing. Don't let that be us. God loves us with a perfect love. In Him, we have everything we need to run this race. We should be living this life to live again, and while we have breath in our bodies, we are to press toward the mark for the prize of the high calling which is in Christ Jesus.

I wonder if we can go to hell for burying what God has invested in us. Hmm…the evil servant did! Let's say it together: "**Jesus, we repent.** We just want to please You. Pour us out, and use us for Your glory!"

From this day forward, see yourself doing what God called you to do. See yourself operating in the anointing God placed on your life. Then get laser focused. Let every decision and step you take be centered in the will of God and in the direction of accomplishing the thing in which God created you to do. **DIE EMPTY!**

Now let's get to work…

ABOUT THE AUTHOR

Donna Casey was born in St. Louis, Missouri. At the age of twenty, she decided to give her life to Jesus and became a spirit-filled believer. She was born into the kingdom under the leadership of the late Pastor Elmer Kirksey Sr. and Assistant Pastor Charles Cummings at Christ Temple on the Rock. Over the years, she served on the praise and worship team, served as assistant to the director of evangelism and assistant director of the women's ministry. She has also been mentored and used greatly in the areas of intercessory prayer, deliverance, and spiritual warfare. Her passion is to minister to all people (including leaders) who are hurt, broken, and lost as described in Isaiah 61:1–3, which was the scripture the Lord gave her when He called Donna into the ministry. She prayed early on that God would give her spiritual insight, and she guards it fiercely as she uses it to help the people of God.

Donna has been under the leadership of Apostle Larry J. Baylor and Dr. Marlon T. Baylor for the last eleven years at Faith Miracle Temple Church where her and her husband, Christopher, serve in ministry together.

CPSIA information can be obtained
at www.ICGtesting.com
Printed in the USA
BVHW071511240121
598545BV00002B/13

9 781098 055035